PENGUIN BOOKS

# FRIENDS IN SMALL PLACES

Ruskin Bond's first novel, *The Room on the Roof*, written when he was seventeen, received the John Llewellyn Rhys Memorial Prize in 1957. Since then he has written a number of novellas, essays, poems and children's books, many of which have been published by Penguin. He has also written over 500 short stories and articles that have appeared in magazines and anthologies. He received the Sahitya Akademi Award in 1992, the Padma Shri in 1999 and the Padma Bhushan in 2014.

Ruskin Bond was born in Kasauli, Himachal Pradesh, and grew up in Jamnagar, Dehradun, New Delhi and Simla. As a young man, he spent four years in the Channel Islands and London. He returned to India in 1955. He now lives in Landour, Mussoorie, with his adopted family.

# *friends in small places*
### *ruskin bond's unforgettable people*

# RUSKIN BOND

PENGUIN BOOKS

An imprint of Penguin Random House

## PENGUIN BOOKS

USA | Canada | UK | Ireland | Australia
New Zealand | India | South Africa | China | Singapore

Puffin Books is part of the Penguin Random House group of companies
whose addresses can be found at global.penguinrandomhouse.com

Published by Penguin Random House India Pvt. Ltd
4th Floor, Capital Tower 1, MG Road,
Gurugram 122 002, Haryana, India

First published by Penguin Books India 2000

24 23 22 20 19 18

ISBN 9780141004297

Typeset in Sabon by Mantra Virtual Services, New Delhi

Printed at Repro India Limited

www.penguin.co.in

# Contents

# Introduction

Meet some of the people I can never forget. Not because they were of great importance or stature but because their individuality made them stand out from the commonplace. It was not money or success but pride in themselves that set them apart. People like my Granny, or my father, or the old kitemaker, or the wayside station's khilasi, or the epileptic boy who sold trinkets for a living.

I've been writing stories of one kind or another for nearly fifty years and, along the way, it has always been the people I've known and met who have given me these stories—friends, lovers, relatives, chance acquaintances, strangers, or other people's friends and relatives. No two persons are alike, although I do believe each of us has a double somewhere. I know I have. There was this lady who came up to me the other day and exclaimed, 'How nice to see you after all these years! But why did you abandon me on the platform at Zurich just after our engagement had been announced?' I hastened to assure her that I had never been to Zurich in my life, and made a quick getaway before she decided I would do instead of my double.

viii      Friends in Small Places

Somerset Maugham liked writing stories about the people he met. So did Maupassant and Chekhov. That's why their stories are never dull. They wrote about real people.

I find most people interesting. The dull ones are those whose lives are a little too orderly, or who are forever boasting of the ease with which they have succeeded in life. Such people can be a little suspect. I used to envy —, who did everything just right, both as a boy and as a man; he never seemed to fail at anything he undertook. When we were Boy Scouts, he could tie all the knots, and I couldn't tie one. And when he was fifty he was still good at tying knots. He bought a rope and hanged himself—as neatly as he had done everything else in life.

Yes, life is full of surprises. And so are people, in their different ways.

And here I'd like to mention and pay tribute to some of the people who do not appear in the stories that follow.

I remember Mr Jones. He was only a junior master at my school in Shimla, where most of his colleagues looked upon him with a certain amusement tinged with disdain, for he was one of those rare people at the time—a teacher who did not believe in corporal punishment and who refused to administer it. Fifty years ago, flogging was still the order of the day, specially in boarding schools. 'Six of the best' with a stout malacca cane was the punishment meted out to those who broke the rules. What was good for Tom Brown at Rugby was good for R. Bond and Singh in Class VII at B.C.S. Most teachers, even some prefects, were expected to cane the boys under their care or command, and many of them did so with sadistic enthusiasm. Not so Mr Jones. He refused to cane anyone. As a result he was considered soft and old-fashioned although he was really ahead of his time. And his principled stand resulted in a loss of seniority and the chance of rising to any heights in the school hierarchy. Then, as now, if you bucked the system, you were made to pay for it.

Not that this bothered Mr Jones. A simple Welshman who had fought in the trenches during the First World War, 'Taffy' Jones had seen real suffering at first-hand and saw no merit in inflicting pain on anyone—least of all on a schoolboy. It made no sense to him. A bachelor all his life, he kept pigeons and a mongrel dog, scorning fancy breeds. As his room was tucked away in a remote corner of the school estate, no one could object to his pets.

On holidays, I would call on him to borrow books. He had a complete set of Dickens, and lent the volumes to me one at a time, until (over a period of two school terms), I had gone through the entire works, from *Sketches by Boz* to *Our Mutual Friend*. Reading became my religion; authorship my goal.

Intellectual nourishment and stimulation are important to a budding writer; but so is physical nourishment. And living on my own in London when I was in my late teens, I soon grew very thin indeed. Subsisting on a diet of beans on toast in coffee bars, I was a prime candidate for malnutrition and lost all vision in my right eye. My own efforts at cooking were limited to boiling eggs. One day I shall write a best-selling cookbook. *Fifty Different Ways to Boil an Egg and Other Disasters*.

You can imagine how glad I was to get back to India, even if it was only to a rented room in Dehra Dun. Here my landlady, Mrs Singh, did at least cook for me, apart from telling me wonderful stories of the supernatural. For breakfast she gave me stuffed mooli (radish) parathas, with a variety of home-made pickles, shalgam (turnip) pickle being my favourite. She also made an excellent kanji (spiced carrot water), which seemed to help my little grey cells work overtime. English literature was all very well; but I needed Indian cooking to help create it. Those two years in Dehra, struggling to establish myself as a writer on Mrs Singh's kanji and the occasional fifty-rupee money order, were probably the most memorable of my life.

I was young, I was courteous, I was on my own, and I looked vulnerable. My friends' mothers, wives, cousins, sisters, aunts, all wanted to keep me from starving.

And still do.

Although I am well spoilt by Prem and his family, who have nurtured me for twenty-five years, there are other good souls who see to it that I do not fade from view: Ganesh Saili and his patient wife and good-hearted daughters; Maya and Victor Banerjee, who spoil me with bacon rashers and liver paté; Reeta and Jeet, who stuff me with various kinds of fish, including (I suspect) a goldfish; Nandu Jauhar, who grows the most delicious mushrooms, in the Savoy ballroom; Upendra Arora, who believes that authors are at their best after a good breakfast; Bill Aitken and H.H. Maharani Sahiba of Jind, who stimulate in more ways than one; and the

Japanese lady who sent me a food parcel, having read somewhere that the wolf was at my door.

Now she knows that I was the wolf.

All these good people, and many others whom I shall thank in person, have contributed to my welfare and seen to it that I am no longer the scrawny, underfed young writer of yesteryear.

I take this opportunity to thank them. May they prosper and continue in their generous ways.

Landour, Mussoorie          *RUSKIN BOND*
December 2000

# Masterji

I was strolling along the platform, waiting for the arrival of the Amritsar Express, when I saw Mr Khushal, handcuffed to a policeman.

I hadn't recognized him at first—a paunchy gentleman with a lot of grey in his beard and a certain arrogant amusement in his manner. It was only when I came closer, and we were almost face to face, that I recognized my old Hindi teacher.

Startled, I stopped and stared. And he stared back at me, a glimmer of recognition in his eyes. It was over twenty years since I'd last seen him, standing jauntily before the classroom blackboard, and now here he was tethered to a policeman and looking as jaunty as ever . . .

'Good—good evening, sir,' I stammered, in my best public school manner. (You must always respect your teacher, no matter what the circumstances.)

Mr Khushal's face lit up with pleasure. 'So you remember me! It's nice to see you again, my boy.'

Forgetting that his right hand was shackled to the policeman's left, I made as if to shake hands. Mr Khushal thoughtfully took my right hand in his left and gave it a rough squeeze. A faint odour of cloves and cinnamon reached me, and I remembered how he had always been redolent of spices when standing beside my desk, watching me agonize over my Hindi-English translation.

He had joined the school in 1948, not long after the Partition. Until then there had been no Hindi teacher; we'd been taught Urdu and French. Then came a ruling that Hindi was to be a compulsory subject, and at the age of sixteen I found myself struggling with a new script. When Mr Khushal joined the staff (on the recommendation of a local official), there was no one else in the school who knew Hindi, or who could assess Mr Khushal's abilities as a teacher . . .

And now once again he stood before me, only this time he was in the custody of the law.

I was still recovering from the shock when the train drew in, and everyone on the platform began making a rush for the compartment doors. As the policeman elbowed his way through the crowd, I kept close behind him and his charge, and as a result I managed to get into the same third-class compartment. I found a seat right opposite Mr Khushal. He did not seem to be the least bit embarrassed by the handcuffs, or by the stares of his fellow-passengers. Rather, it was the policeman who looked unhappy and ill at ease.

As the train got under way, I offered Mr Khushal one of the parathas made for me by my Ferozepur landlady. He accepted it with alacrity. I offered one to the constable as well, but although he looked at it with undisguised longing, he felt duty-bound to decline.

'Why have they arrested you, sir?' I asked. 'Is it very serious?'

'A trivial matter,' said Mr Khushal. 'Nothing to worry about. I shall be at liberty soon.'

'But what did you do?'

Mr Khushal leant forward. 'Nothing to be ashamed of,' he said in a confiding tone. 'Even a great teacher like Socrates fell foul of the law.'

'You mean—one of your pupil's—made a complaint?'

'And why should one of my pupils make a complaint?' Mr Khushal looked offended. 'They were the beneficiaries—it was for *them*.' He noticed that I looked mystified, and decided to come straight to the point, 'It was simply a question of false certificates.'

'Oh,' I said, feeling deflated. Public school boys are always prone to jump to the wrong conclusions . . .

'*Your* certificates, sir?'

'Of course not. Nothing wrong with my certificates—I had them printed in Lahore, in 1946.'

'With age comes respectability,' I remarked. 'In that case, whose . . .?'

'Why, the matriculation certificates I've been providing all these years to the poor idiots who would never have got through on their own!'

'You mean you gave them your own certificates?'

'That's right. And if it hadn't been for so many printing mistakes, no one would have been any wiser. You can't find a good press these days, that's the trouble . . . It was a public service, my boy, I hope you appreciate that . . . It isn't fair to hold a boy back in life simply because he can't get through some puny exam . . . Mind you, I don't give my certificates to *anyone*. They come to me only after they have failed two or three times.'

'And I suppose you charge something?'

'Only if they can pay. There's no fixed sum. Whatever they like to give me. I've never been greedy in these matters, and you know I am not unkind . . .'

Which is true enough, I thought, looking out of the carriage window at the green fields of Moga and remembering the half-yearly Hindi exam when I had stared blankly at the question paper, knowing that I was totally incapable of answering any of it. Mr Khushal had come walking down the line of desks and stopped at mine, breathing cloves all over me. 'Come on, boy, why haven't you started?'

'Can't do it, sir,' I'd said. 'It's too difficult.'

'Never mind,' he'd urged in a whisper. 'Do *something*. Copy it out, copy it out!'

And so, to pass the time, I'd copied out the entire paper, word for word. And a fortnight later, when the results were out, I found I had passed!

'But, sir,' I had stammered, approaching Mr Khushal when I found him alone, 'I never answered the paper. I couldn't translate the passage. All I did was copy it out!'

'That's why I gave you pass marks,' he'd answered imperturbably. 'You have such a neat handwriting. If ever you *do* learn Hindi, my boy, you'll write a beautiful script!'

And remembering that moment, I was now filled

with compassion for my old teacher; and leaning across, I placed my hand on his knee and said, 'Sir, if they convict you, I hope it won't be for long. And when you come out, if you happen to be in Delhi or Ferozepur, please look me up. You see, I'm still rather hopeless at Hindi, and perhaps you could give me tuition. I'd be glad to pay . . .'

Mr Khushal threw back his head and laughed, and the entire compartment shook with his laughter.

'Teach you Hindi!' he cried. 'My dear boy, what gave you the idea that I ever knew any Hindi?'

'But, sir—if not Hindi, what were you teaching us all the time at school?'

'Punjabi!' he shouted, and everyone jumped in their seats. 'Pure Punjabi! But how were *you* to know the difference?'

# Keemat Lal

I met Inspector Keemat Lal about two years ago, while I was living in the hot, dusty town of Shahpur in the plains of northern India.

Keemat Lal had charge of the local police station. He was a heavily built man, slow and rather ponderous, and inclined to be lazy; but, like most lazy people, he was intelligent. He was also a failure. He had remained an inspector for a number of years, and had given up all hope of further promotion. His luck was against him, he said. He should never have been a policeman. He had been born under the sign of Capricorn and should really have gone into the restaurant business but now it was too late to do anything about it.

The Inspector and I had little in common. He was nearing forty, and I was twenty-five. But both of us spoke English, and in Shahpur there were very few people who did. In addition, we were both fond of beer. There were no places of entertainment in Shahpur. The searing heat, the dust that came whirling up from the east, the mosquitoes (almost as

---

The story originally appeared as *A Case For Inspector Lal*

numerous as the flies), and the general monotony gave one a thirst for something more substantial than stale lemonade.

My house was on the outskirts of the town, where we were not often disturbed. On two or three evenings in the week, just as the sun was going down and making it possible for one to emerge from the khas-cooled confines of a dark, high-ceilinged bedroom, Inspector Keemat Lal would appear on the veranda steps, mopping the sweat from his face with a small towel, which he used instead of a handkerchief. My only servant, excited at the prospect of serving an inspector of police, would hurry out with glasses, a bucket of ice and several bottles of the best Indian beer.

One evening, after we had overtaken our fourth bottle, I said, 'You must have had some interesting cases in your career, Inspector.'

'Most of them were rather dull,' he said. 'At least the successful ones were. The sensational cases usually went unsolved—otherwise I might have been a superintendent by now. I suppose you are talking of murder cases. Do you remember the shooting of the minister of the interior? I was on that one, but it was a political murder and we never solved it.'

'Tell me about a case you solved,' I said. 'An interesting one.' When I saw him looking uncomfortable, I added, 'You don't have to worry, Inspector. I'm a very discreet person, in spite of all the beer I consume.'

'But how can you be discreet? You are a writer.'

I protested, 'Writers are usually very discreet. They always change the names of people and places.'

He gave me one of his rare smiles. 'And how would you describe me, if you were to put me into a story?'

'Oh, I'd leave you as you are. No one would believe in you, anyway.'

He laughed indulgently and poured out more beer. 'I suppose I can change names, too . . . I will tell you of a very interesting case. The victim was an unusual person, and so was the killer. But you must promise not to write this story.'

'I promise,' I lied.

'Do you know Panauli?'

'In the hills? Yes, I have been there once or twice.'

'Good, then you will follow me without my

having to be too descriptive. This happened about three years ago, shortly after I had been stationed at Panauli. Nothing much ever happened there. There were a few cases of theft and cheating, and an occasional fight during the summer. A murder took place about once every ten years. It was therefore quite an event when the Rani of —— was found dead in her sitting room, her head split open with an axe. I knew that I would have to solve the case if I wanted to stay in Panauli.

'The trouble was, anyone could have killed the Rani, and there were some who made no secret of their satisfaction that she was dead. She had been an unpopular woman. Her husband was dead, her children were scattered, and her money—for she had never been a very wealthy Rani—had been dwindling away. She lived alone in an old house on the outskirts of the town, ruling the locality with the stern authority of a matriarch. She had a servant, and he was the man who found the body and came to the police, dithering and tongue-tied. I arrested him at once, of course. I knew he was probably innocent, but a basic rule is to grab the first man on the scene of crime, specially if he happens to be a servant. But we let him go after a beating. There was nothing much he could tell us, and he had a sound alibi.

'The axe with which the Rani had been killed must have been a small woodcutter's axe—so we deduced from the wound. We couldn't find the weapon. It might have been used by a man or a woman, and there were several of both sexes who had a grudge against the Rani. There were bazaar rumours that she had been supplementing her income by trafficking in young women: she had the necessary connections. There were also rumours that she possessed vast wealth, and that it was stored away in her godowns. We did not find any treasure. There were so many rumours darting about like battered shuttlecocks that I decided to stop wasting my time in trying to follow them up. Instead, I restricted my inquiries to those people who had been close to the Rani—either in their personal relationships or in actual physical proximity.

'To begin with, there was Mr Kapur, a wealthy businessman from Bombay who had a house in Panauli. He was supposed to be an old admirer of the Rani's. I discovered that he had occasionally lent her money, and that, in spite of his professed friendship for her, he had charged a high rate of interest.

'Then there were her immediate neighbours—an American missionary and his wife, who had been trying to convert the Rani to Christianity; an English spinster of seventy who made no secret of the fact that she and the Rani hated each other with great enthusiasm; a local councillor and his family, who did not get on well with their aristocratic neighbour; and a tailor, who kept his shop close by. None of these people had any powerful motive for killing the Rani—or none that I could discover. But the tailor's daughter interested me.

'Her name was Kusum. She was twelve or thirteen years old—a thin, dark girl, with lovely black eyes and a swift, disarming smile. While I was making my routine inquiries in the vicinity of the Rani's house, I noticed that the girl always tried to avoid me. When I questioned her about the Rani, and about her own movements on the day of the crime, she pretended to be very vague and stupid.

'But I could see she was not stupid, and I became convinced that she knew something unusual about the Rani. She might even know something about the murder. She could have been protecting someone, and was afraid to tell me what she knew. Often, when I spoke to her of the violence of the Rani's death, I saw fear in her eyes. I began to think the girl's life might be in danger, and I had a close watch kept on her. I liked her. I liked her youth and freshness, and the innocence and wonder in her eyes. I spoke to her whenever I could, kindly and paternally, and though I knew she rather liked me and found me amusing—the ups and downs of Panauli always left me panting for breath—and though I could see that she *wanted* to tell me something, she always held back at the last moment.

'Then, one afternoon while I was in the Rani's house going through her effects, I saw something glistening in a narrow crack near the doorstep. I would not have noticed it if the sun had not been pouring through the window, glinting off the little object. I stooped and picked up a piece of glass. It was part of a broken bangle.

'I turned the fragment over in my hand. There was something familiar about its colour and design. Didn't Kusum wear similar glass bangles? I went to look for the girl but she was not at her father's shop. I was told that she had gone down the hill, to gather firewood.

'I decided to take the narrow path down the hill. It went round some rocks and cactus, and then disappeared into a forest of oak trees. I found Kusum sitting at the edge of the forest, a bundle of twigs beside her.

'"You are always wandering about alone," I said. "Don't you feel afraid?"

'"It is safer when I am alone," she replied. "Nobody comes here."

'I glanced quickly at the bangles on her wrist, and noticed that their colour matched that of the broken piece. I held out the bit of broken glass and said, "I found it in the Rani's house. It must have fallen . . ."

'She did not wait for me to finish what I was saying. With a look of terror, she sprang up from the grass and fled into the forest.

'I was completely taken aback. I had not expected such a reaction. Of what significance was the broken bangle? I hurried after the girl, slipping on the smooth pine needles that covered the slopes. I was searching amongst the trees when I heard someone sobbing behind me. When I turned round, I saw the girl standing on a boulder, facing me with an axe in her hands.

'When Kusum saw me staring at her, she raised the axe and rushed down the slope towards me.

'I was too bewildered to be able to do anything but stare with open mouth as she rushed at me with the axe. The impetus of her run would have brought her right up against me, and the axe, coming down, would probably have crushed my skull, thick though it is. But while she was still six feet from me, the axe flew out of her hands. It sprang into the air as though it had a life of its own and came curving towards me.

'In spite of my weight, I moved swiftly aside. The axe grazed my shoulder and sank into the soft bark of the tree behind me. And Kusum dropped at my feet weeping hysterically.'

Inspector Keemat Lal paused in order to replenish his glass. He took a long pull at the beer and the froth glistened on his moustache.

'And then what happened?' I prompted him.

'Perhaps it could only have happened in India—and to a person like me,' he said. 'This sudden compassion for the person you are supposed to destroy. Instead of being furious and outraged, instead of seizing the girl and marching her off to the police station, I stroked her head and said silly comforting things.'

'And she told you that she had killed the Rani?'

'She told me how the Rani had called her to her house and given her tea and sweets. Mr Kapur had been there. After some time he began stroking Kusum's arms and squeezing her knees. She had drawn away, but Kapur kept pawing her. The Rani was telling Kusum not to be afraid, that no harm would come to her. Kusum slipped away from the man and made a rush for the door. The Rani caught her by the shoulders and pushed her back into the room. The Rani was getting angry. Kusum saw the axe lying in a corner of the room. She seized it, raised it above her head and threatened Kapur. The man realized that he had gone too far, and, valuing his neck, backed away. But the Rani, in a great rage, sprang at the girl. And Kusum, in desperation and panic, brought the axe down across the Rani's head.'

'The Rani fell to the ground. Without waiting to see what Kapur might do, Kusum fled from the house. Her bangle must have broken when she stumbled against the door. She ran into the forest and, after concealing the axe amongst some tall ferns, lay weeping on the grass until it grew dark.

But such was her nature, and such the resilience of youth, that she recovered sufficiently to be able to return home looking her normal self. And during the following days she managed to remain silent about the whole business.'

'What did you do about it?' I asked.

Keemat Lal looked me straight in my beery eye. 'Nothing,' he said. 'I did absolutely nothing. I couldn't have the girl put away in a remand home. It would have crushed her spirit.'

'And what about Kapur?'

'Oh, he had his own reasons for remaining quiet, as you may guess. No, the case was closed—or perhaps I should say the file was put in my pending tray. My promotion, too, went into the pending tray.'

'It didn't turn out very well for you,' I said.

'No. Here I am in Shahpur, and still an inspector. But, tell me, what would you have done if you had been in my place?'

I considered his question carefully for a moment or two, then said, 'I suppose it would have depended on how much sympathy the girl evoked in me. She had killed in innocence . . .'

'Then you would have put your personal feeling

above your duty to uphold the law?'

'Yes. But I would not have made a very good policeman.'

'Exactly.'

'Still, it's a pity that Kapur got off so easily.'

'There was no alternative if I was to let the girl go. But he didn't get off altogether. He found himself in trouble later on for swindling some manufacturing concern, and went to jail for a couple of years.'

'And the girl—did you see her again?'

'Well, before I was transferred from Panauli, I saw her occasionally on the road. She was usually on her way to school. She would greet me with folded hands, and call me Uncle.'

The beer bottles were all empty, and Inspector Keemat Lal got up to leave. His final words to me were, 'I should never have been a policeman.'

# Kishan Singh

About fifty feet from the entrance to the tunnel stood the watchman's hut. Marigolds grew in front of the hut, and at the back, there was a small vegetable patch. It was the watchman's duty to inspect the tunnel and keep it clear of obstacles.

Every day, before the train came through, he would walk the length of the tunnel. If all was well, he would return to his hut and take a nap. If something was wrong, he would walk back up the line and wave a red flag and the engine driver would slow down.

At night, the watchman lit an oil lamp and made a similar inspection. If there was any danger to the train, he'd go back up the line and wave his lamp to the approaching engine. If all was well, he'd hang his lamp at the door of his hut and go to sleep.

He was just settling down on his cot for an afternoon nap when he saw the boy come out of the tunnel. He waited until the boy was only a few feet away and then said, 'Welcome, welcome. I don't often get visitors. Sit down for a while, and tell me

Extract from *The Tunnel*

why you were inspecting my tunnel.'

'Is it your tunnel?' asked Ranji.

'It is,' said the watchman. 'It is truly my tunnel, since no one else will have anything to do with it. I have only lent it to the Government.'

Ranji sat down on the edge of the cot.

'I wanted to see the train come through,' he said. 'And then, when it had gone, I decided to walk through the tunnel.'

'And what did you find in it?'

'Nothing. It was very dark. But when I came out, I thought I saw an animal—up on the hill—but I'm not sure, it moved off very quickly.'

'It was a leopard you saw,' said the watchman. 'My leopard.'

'Do you own a leopard too?'

'I do.'

'And do you lend it to the Government?'

'I do not.'

'Is it dangerous?'

'Not if you leave it alone. It comes this way for a few days every month, because there are still deer in this jungle, and the deer is its natural prey. It keeps away from people.'

'Have you been here a long time?' asked Ranji.

'Many years. My name is Kishan Singh.'

'Mine is Ranji.'

'There is one train during the day. And there is one train during the night. Have you seen the Night Mail come through the tunnel?'

'No. At what time does it come?'

'About nine o'clock, if it isn't late. You could come and sit here with me, if you like. And after it has gone I will take you home.'

'I'll ask my parents,' said Ranji. 'Will it be safe?'

'It is safer in the jungle than in the town. No rascals out here. Only last week, when I went into the town, I had my pocket picked! Leopards don't pick pockets.'

Kishan Singh stretched himself out on his cot. 'And now I am going to take a nap, my friend. It is too hot to be up and about in the afternoon.'

'Everyone goes to sleep in the afternoon,' complained Ranji. 'My father lies down as soon as he's had his lunch.'

'Well, the animals also rest in the heat of the day. It is only the tribe of boys who cannot, or will not, rest.'

Kishan Singh placed a large banana leaf over his face to keep away the flies, and was soon snoring gently. Ranji stood up, looking up and down the railway tracks. Then he began walking back to the village.

The following evening, towards dusk, as the flying foxes swooped silently out of the trees, Ranji made his way to the watchman's hut.

It had been a long hot day, but now the earth was cooling and a light breeze was moving through the trees. It carried with it the scent of mango blossom, the promise of rain.

Kishan Singh was waiting for Ranji. He had watered his small garden and the flowers looked cool and fresh. A kettle was boiling on an oil stove.

'I am making tea,' he said. 'There is nothing like a glass of hot sweet tea while waiting for a train.'

They drank their tea, listening to the sharp notes of the tailor-bird and the noisy chatter of the seven-sisters. As the brief twilight faded, most of the birds fell silent. Kishan lit his oil lamp and said it was time for him to inspect the tunnel. He moved off towards the dark entrance, while Ranji sat on the cot, sipping tea.

In the dark, the trees seemed to move closer. And the night life of the forest was conveyed on the

breeze—the sharp call of a barking-deer, the cry of a
fox, the quaint tonk-tonk of a nightjar.

There were some sounds that Ranji would not
recognize—sounds that came from the trees.
Creakings, and whisperings, as though the trees
were coming alive, stretching their limbs in the
dark, shifting a little, flexing their fingers.

Kishan Singh stood outside the tunnel, trimming
his lamp. The night sounds were familiar to him and
he did not give them much thought; but something
else—a padded footfall, a rustle of dry
leaves—made him stand still for a few seconds,
peering into the darkness. Then, humming softly, he
returned to where Ranji was waiting. Ten minutes
remained for the Night Mail to arrive.

As the watchman sat down on the cot beside
Ranji, a new sound reached both of them quite
distinctly—a rhythmic sawing sound, as of someone
cutting through the branch of a tree.

'What's that?' whispered Ranji.

'It's the leopard,' said Kishan Singh. 'I think it's
in the tunnel.'

'The train will soon be here.'

'Yes, my friend. And if we don't drive the
leopard out of the tunnel, it will be run over by

the engine.'

'But won't it attack us if we try to drive it out?' asked Ranji, beginning to share the watchman's concern.

'It knows me well. We have seen each other many times. I don't think it will attack. Even so, I will take my axe along. You had better stay here, Ranji.'

'No, I'll come too. It will be better than sitting here alone in the dark.'

'All right, but stay close behind me. And, remember, there is nothing to fear.'

Raising his lamp, Kishan Singh walked into the tunnel, shouting at the top of his voice to try and scare away the animal. Ranji followed close behind. But he found he was unable to do any shouting; his throat had gone quite dry.

They had gone about twenty paces into the tunnel when the light from the lamp fell upon the leopard. It was crouching between the tracks, only fifteen feet away from them. Baring its teeth and snarling, it went down on its belly, tail twitching. Ranji felt sure it was going to spring at them.

Kishan Singh and Ranji both shouted together. Their voices rang through the tunnel. And the leopard, uncertain as to how many terrifying humans were there in front of him, turned swiftly and disappeared into the darkness.

To make sure it had gone, Ranji and the watchman walked the length of the tunnel. When they returned to the entrance, the rails were beginning to hum. They knew the train was coming.

Ranji put his hand to one of the rails and felt its tremor. He heard the distant rumble of the train. And then the engine came round the bend, hissing at them, scattering sparks into the darkness, defying the jungle as it roared through the steep sides of the cutting. It charged straight into the tunnel, thundering past Ranji like the beautiful dragon of his dreams.

And when it had gone, the silence returned and the forest seemed to breathe, to live again. Only the rails still trembled with the passing of the train.

They trembled again to the passing of the same train, almost a week later, when Ranji and his father were both travelling in it.

Ranji's father was scribbling in a notebook, doing his accounts. How boring of him, thought Ranji as he sat near an open window staring out at the darkness. His father was going to Delhi on a business trip and had decided to take the boy along.

'It's time you learnt something about the business,' he had said, to Ranji's dismay.

The Night Mail rushed through the forest with its hundreds of passengers. The carriage wheels beat out a steady rhythm on the rails. Tiny flickering lights came and went, as they passed small villages on the fringe of the jungle.

Ranji heard the rumble as the train passed over a small bridge. It was too dark to see the hut near the cutting, but he knew they must be approaching the tunnel. He strained his eyes, looking out into the night; and then, just as the engine let out a shrill whistle, Ranji saw the lamp.

He couldn't see Kishan Singh, but he saw the lamp, and he knew that his friend was out there.

The train went into the tunnel and out again, it left the jungle behind and thundered across the endless plains. And Ranji stared out at the darkness, thinking of the lonely cutting in the forest, and the watchman with the lamp who would always remain a firefly for those travelling thousands, as he lit up the darkness for steam engines and leopards.

# Dukhi and the Maharani

We lived in an old palace beside a lake. The palace looked like a ruin from the outside, but the rooms were cool and comfortable. We lived in one wing, and my father organized a small school in another wing. His pupils were the children of the Raja and the Raja's relatives. My father had started life in India as a tea planter, but he had been trained as a teacher and the idea of starting a school in a small state facing the Arabian Sea had appealed to him. The pay wasn't much, but we had a palace to live in, the latest 1938-model Hillman to drive about in, and a number of servants. In those days, of course, everyone had servants (although the servants did not have any!). Ayah was our own; but the cook, the bearer, the gardener, and the bhisti were all provided by the state.

Sometimes I sat in the schoolroom with the other children (who were all much bigger than me), sometimes I remained in the house with Ayah, sometimes I followed the gardener, Dukhi, about the spacious garden.

---

Extract from *A Room of Many Colours*

Dukhi means 'sad', and though I never could discover if the gardener had anything to feel sad about, the name certainly suited him. He had grown to resemble the drooping weeds that he was always digging up with a tiny spade. I seldom saw him standing up. He always sat on the ground with his knees well up to his chin, and attacked the weeds from this position. He could spend all day on his haunches, moving about the garden simply by shuffling his feet along the grass.

I tried to imitate his posture, sitting down on my heels and putting my knees into my armpits, but could never hold the position for more than five minutes.

Time had no meaning in a large garden, and Dukhi never hurried. Life, for him, was not a matter of one year succeeding another, but of five seasons—winter, spring, hot weather, monsoon and autumn—arriving and departing. His seedbeds had always to be in readiness for the coming season, and he did not look any further than the next monsoon. It was impossible to tell his age. He may have been thirty-six or eighty-six. He was either very young for his years or very old for them.

Dukhi loved bright colours, specially reds and

yellows. He liked strongly scented flowers, like jasmine and honeysuckle. He couldn't understand my father's preference for the more delicately perfumed petunias and sweet peas. But I shared Dukhi's fondness for the common bright orange marigold, which is offered in temples and is used to make garlands and nosegays. When the garden was bare of all colour, the marigold would still be there, gay and flashy, challenging the sun.

Dukhi was very fond of making nosegays, and I liked to watch him at work. A sunflower formed the centrepiece. It was surrounded by roses, marigolds and oleander, fringed with green leaves, and bound together with silver thread. The perfume was overpowering. The nosegays were presented to me or my father on special occasions, that is, on a birthday or to guests of my father's who were considered important.

One day I found Dukhi making a nosegay, and said, 'No one is coming today, Dukhi. It isn't even a birthday.'

'It is a birthday, chhota sahib,' he said. 'Little sahib' was the title he had given me. It wasn't much of a title compared to Raja sahib, Diwan sahib or Burra sahib, but it was nice to have a title at the age of seven.

'Oh,' I said. 'And is there a party, too?'

'No party.'

'What's the use of a birthday without a party? What's the use of a birthday without presents?'

'This person doesn't like presents—just flowers.'

'Who is it?' I asked, full of curiosity.

'If you want to find out, you can take these flowers to her. She lives right at the top of that far side of the palace. There are twenty-two steps to climb. Remember that, chhota sahib, you take twenty-three steps and you will go over the edge and into the lake!'

I started climbing the stairs.

It was a spiral staircase of wrought iron, and it went round and round and up and up, and it made me quite dizzy and tired.

At the top, I found myself on a small balcony, which looked out over the lake and another palace; at the crowded city and the distant harbour. I heard a voice, a rather high, musical voice, saying (in English), 'Are you a ghost?' I turned to see who had spoken but found the balcony empty. The voice had come from a dark room.

I turned to the stairway, ready to flee, but the voice said, 'Oh, don't go, there's nothing to be frightened of!'

And so I stood still, peering cautiously into the darkness of the room.

'First, tell me—are you a ghost?'

'I'm a boy,' I said.

'And I'm a girl. We can be friends. I can't come out there, so you had better come in. Come along, I'm not a ghost either—not yet, anyway!'

As there was nothing very frightening about the voice, I stepped into the room. It was dark inside, and, coming in from the glare, it took me some time to make out the tiny, elderly lady seated on a cushioned gilt chair. She wore a red sari, lots of coloured bangles on her wrists, and golden earrings. Her hair was streaked with white, but her skin was still quite smooth and unlined, and she had large and very beautiful eyes.

'You must be Master Bond!' she said. 'Do you know who I am?'

'You're a lady with a birthday,' I said, 'but that's all I know. Dukhi didn't tell me any more.'

'If you promise to keep it a secret, I'll tell you who I am. You see, everyone thinks I'm mad. Do you think so too?'

'I don't know.'

'Well, you must tell me if you think so,' she said with a chuckle. Her laugh was the sort of sound made by the gecko, a little wall-lizard, coming from deep down in the throat. 'I have a feeling you are a truthful boy. Do you find it very difficult to tell the truth?'

'Sometimes.'

'Sometimes. Of course, there are times when I tell lies—lots of little lies—because they're such fun! But would you call me a liar? I wouldn't, if I were you, but *would* you?'

'Are you a liar?'

'I'm asking you! If I were to tell you that I was a queen—that I *am* a queen—would you believe me?'

I thought deeply about this, and then said, 'I'll try to believe you.'

'Oh, but you must believe me. I'm a real queen, I'm a Rani! Look, I've got diamonds to prove it!' And she held out her hands, and there was a ring on each finger, the stones glowing and glittering in the dim light. 'Diamonds, rubies, pearls and emeralds! Only a queen can have these!' She was most anxious that I should believe her.

'You must be a queen,' I said.

'Right!' she snapped. 'In that case, would you mind calling me "Your Highness"?'

'Your Highness,' I said.

She smiled. It was a slow, beautiful smile. Her whole face lit up.

'I could love you,' she said. 'But better still, I'll give you something to eat. Do you like chocolates?'

'Yes, Your Highness.'

'Well,' she said, taking a box from the table beside her, 'these have come all the way from England. Take two. Only two, mind, otherwise the box will finish before Thursday, and I don't want that to happen because I won't get any more till Saturday. That's when Captain MacWhirr's ship gets in, the *S.S. Lucy*, loaded with boxes and boxes of chocolates!'

'All for you?' I asked in considerable awe.

'Yes, of course. They have to last at least three months. I get them from England. I get only the best chocolates. I like them with pink, crunchy fillings, don't you?'

'Oh, yes!' I exclaimed, full of envy.

'Never mind,' she said. 'I may give you one, now and then—if you're *very* nice to me! Here you are, help yourself . . .' She pushed the chocolate box towards me.

I took a silver-wrapped chocolate, and then just as I was thinking of taking a second, she quickly took the box away. 'No more!' she said. 'They have to last till Saturday.'

'But I took only *one*,' I said with some indignation.

'Did you?' She gave me a sharp look, decided I was telling the truth, and said graciously, 'Well, in that case, you can have another.'

Watching the Rani carefully, in case she snatched the box away again, I selected a second chocolate, this one with a green wrapper. I don't remember what kind of day it was outside, but I remember the bright green of the chocolate wrapper.

I thought it would be rude to eat the chocolates in front of a queen, so I put them in my pocket and said, 'I'd better go now. Ayah will be looking for me.'

'And when will you be coming to see me again?'

'I don't know,' I said.

'Your Highness.'

'Your Highness.'

'There's something I want you to do for me,' she said, placing one finger on my shoulder and giving me a conspiratorial look. 'Will you do it?'

'What is it, Your Highness?'

'What is it? Why do you ask? A real prince never asks where or why or whatever, he simply does what the princess asks of him. When I was a princess—before I became a queen, that is—I asked a prince to swim across the lake and fetch me a lily growing on the other bank.'

'And did he get it for you?'

'He drowned halfway across. Let that be a lesson to you. Never agree to do something without knowing what it is.'

'But I thought you said . . .'

'Never mind what I *said*. It's what I *say* that matters!'

'Oh, all right,' I said, fidgeting to be gone. 'What is it you want me to do?'

'Nothing.' Her tiny rosebud lips pouted and she stared sullenly at a picture on the wall. Now that my eyes had grown used to the dim light in the room, I noticed that the walls were hung with portraits of stout Rajas and Ranis, turbaned and bedecked in fine clothes. There were also portraits of Queen

Victoria and King George V of England. And, in the centre of all this distinguished company, a large picture of Mickey Mouse.

'I'll do it if it isn't too dangerous,' I said.

'Then listen.' She took my hand and drew me towards her—what a tiny hand she had!—and whispered, 'I want a *red* rose. From the palace garden. But be careful! Don't let Dukhi, the gardener, catch you. He'll know it's for me. He knows I love roses. And he hates me! I'll tell you why, one day. But if he catches you, he'll do something terrible.'

'To me?'

'No, to himself. That's much worse, isn't it? He'll tie himself into knots, or lie naked on a bed of thorns, or go on a long fast with nothing to eat but fruit, sweets and chicken! So you will be careful, won't you?'

'Oh, but he doesn't hate you,' I cried in protest, remembering the flowers he'd sent for her, and looking around I found that I'd been sitting on them. 'Look, he sent these flowers for your birthday!'

'Well, if he sent them for my birthday, you can take them back,' she snapped. 'But if he sent them for *me* . . .' and she suddenly softened and looked coy, 'then I might keep them. Thank you, my dear, it was a very sweet thought.' And she leant forward as though to kiss me.

'It's late, I must go!' I said in alarm, and turning on my heels, ran out of the room and down the spiral staircase.

Father hadn't started lunch, or rather tiffin, as we called it then. He usually waited for me if I was late. I don't suppose he enjoyed eating alone.

'And where have you been?' he asked, helping himself to the rice as soon as he saw me come in.

'To the top of the old palace,' I said.

'Did you meet anyone there?'

'Yes, I met a tiny lady who told me she was a Rani. She gave me chocolates.'

'As a rule, she doesn't like visitors.'

'Oh, she didn't mind me. But is she really a queen?'

'Well, she's the daughter of a Maharaja. That makes her a princess. She never married. There's a story that she fell in love with a commoner, one of the palace servants, and wanted to marry him, but of course they wouldn't allow that. She became very melancholic, and started living all by herself in the old palace. They give her everything she needs, but she doesn't go out or have visitors. Everyone says she's mad.'

'How do they know?' I asked.

'Because she's different from other people, I suppose.'

'Is that being mad?'

'No. Not really. I suppose madness is not *seeing* things as others see them.'

'Is that very bad?'

'No,' said Father, who for once was finding it very difficult to explain something to me. 'But people who are like that—people whose minds are so different that they don't think, step by step, as we do, whose thoughts jump all over the place—such people are very difficult to live with . . .'

One afternoon, while Father was at school, Ayah found a snake in the bathtub. It wasn't early morning and so the snake couldn't have been a lucky one. Ayah was frightened and ran into the garden calling for help. Dukhi came running. Ayah ordered me to stay outside while they went after the snake.

And it was while I was alone in the garden—an unusual circumstance, since Dukhi was nearly always there—that I remembered the Rani's request. On an impulse, I went to the nearest rose bush and plucked the largest rose, pricking my thumb in the process.

And then, without waiting to see what had happened to the snake (it finally escaped), I started up the steps to the top of the old palace.

When I got to the top, I knocked on the door of the Rani's room. Getting no reply, I walked along the balcony until I reached another doorway. There were wooden panels around the door, with elephants, camels and turbaned warriors carved into it. As the door was open, I walked boldly into the room, then stood still in astonishment. The room was filled with a strange light.

There were windows going right round the room, and each small windowpane was made of a different coloured glass. The sun that came through one window flung red and green and purple colours on the figure of the little Rani who stood there with her face pressed to the glass.

She spoke to me without turning from the window. 'This is my favourite room. I have all the colours here. I can see a different world through each pane of glass. Come, join me!' And she beckoned to me, her small hand fluttering like a delicate butterfly.

I went up to the Rani. She was only a little taller than me, and we were able to share the same windowpane.

'See, it's a red world!' she said.

The garden below, the palace and the lake, were all tinted red. I watched the Rani's world for a little while and then touched her on the arm and said, 'I have brought you a rose!'

She started away from me, and her eyes looked frightened. She would not look at the rose.

'Oh, why did you bring it?' she cried, wringing her hands. 'He'll be arrested now!'

'Who'll be arrested?'

'The prince, of course!'

'But *I* took it,' I said. 'No one saw me. Ayah and Dukhi were inside the house, catching a snake.'

'Did they catch it?' she asked, forgetting about the rose.

'I don't know. I didn't wait to see!'

'They should follow the snake, instead of catching it. It may lead them to a treasure. All snakes have treasures to guard.'

This seemed to confirm what Ayah had been telling me, and I resolved that I would follow the next snake that I met.

'Don't you like the rose, then?' I asked.

'Did you steal it?'

'Yes.'

'Good. Flowers should always be stolen. They're more fragrant then.'

Because of a man called Hitler, war had been declared in Europe, and Britain was fighting Germany.

In my comic papers, the Germans were usually shown as blundering idiots; so I didn't see how Britain could possibly lose the war, nor why it should concern India, nor why it should be necessary for my father to join up. But I remember him showing me a newspaper headline which said:

*BOMBS FALL ON BUCKINGHAM PALACE—*
*KING AND QUEEN SAFE*

I expect that had something to do with it.

He went to Delhi for an interview with the RAF

and I was left in Ayah's charge . . .

I had almost forgotten the Rani in the old palace and was about to pay her a visit when, to my surprise, I found her in the garden.

I had risen early that morning, and had gone running barefoot over the dew-drenched grass. No one was about, but I startled a flock of parrots and the birds rose screeching from a banyan tree and wheeled away to some other corner of the palace grounds. I was just in time to see a mongoose scurrying across the grass with an egg in its mouth. The mongoose must have been raiding the poultry farm at the palace.

I was trying to locate the mongoose's hideout, and was on all fours in a jungle of tall cosmos plants when I heard the rustle of clothes, and turned to find the Rani staring at me.

She didn't ask me what I was doing there, but simply said, 'I don't think he could have gone in there.'

'But I saw him go this way,' I said.

'Nonsense! He doesn't live in this part of the garden. He lives in the roots of the banyan tree.'

'But that's where the snake lives,' I said.

'You mean the snake who was a prince. Well,

that's who I'm looking for!'

'A snake who was a prince!' I gaped at the Rani.

She made a gesture of impatience with her butterfly hands, and said, 'Tut, you're only a child, you can't *understand*. The prince lives in the roots of the banyan tree, but he comes out early every morning. Have you seen him?'

'No. But I saw a mongoose.'

The Rani became frightened. 'Oh dear, is there a mongoose in the garden? He might kill the prince!'

'How can a mongoose kill a prince?' I asked.

'You don't understand, Master Bond. Princes, when they die, are born again as snakes.'

'All princes?'

'No, only those who die before they can marry.'

'Did your prince die before he could marry you?'

'Yes. And he returned to this garden in the form of a beautiful snake.'

'Well,' I said, 'I hope it wasn't the snake the water-carrier killed last week.'

'He killed a snake!' The Rani looked horrified. She was quivering all over. 'It might have been the prince!'

'It was a brown snake,' I said.

'Oh, then  it wasn't him.'  She looked very

relieved. 'Brown snakes are only ministers and people like that. It has to be a green snake to be a prince.'

'I haven't seen any green snakes here.'

'There's one living in the roots of the banyan tree. You won't kill it, will you?'

'Not if it's really a prince.'

'And you won't let others kill it?'

'I'll tell Ayah.'

'Good. You're on my side. But be careful of the gardener. Keep him away from the banyan tree. He's always killing snakes. I don't trust him at all.'

She came nearer and, leaning forward a little, looked into my eyes.

'Blue eyes—I trust them. But don't trust green eyes. And yellow eyes are evil.'

'I've never seen yellow eyes.'

'That's because you're pure,' she said, and turned away and hurried across the lawn as though she had just remembered a very urgent appointment.

The sun was up, slanting through the branches of the banyan tree, and Ayah's voice could be heard calling me for breakfast.

'Dukhi,' I said, when I found him in the garden

later that day, 'Dukhi, don't kill the snake in the banyan tree.'

'A snake in the banyan tree!' he exclaimed, seizing his hose.

'No, no!' I said. 'I haven't seen it. But the Rani says there's one. She says it was a prince in its former life, and that we shouldn't kill it.'

'Oh,' said Dukhi, smiling to himself. 'The Rani says so. All right, you tell her we won't kill it.'

'Is it true that she was in love with a prince but that he died before she could marry him?'

'Something like that,' said Dukhi. 'It was a long time ago—before I came here.'

'My father says it wasn't a prince, but a commoner. Are you a commoner, Dukhi?'

'A commoner? What's that, chhota sahib?'

'I'm not sure. Someone very poor, I suppose.'

'Then I must be a commoner,' said Dukhi.

'Were *you* in love with the Rani?' I asked.

Dukhi was so startled that he dropped his hose and lost his balance; the first time I'd seen him lose his poise while squatting on his haunches.

'Don't say such things, chhota sahib!'

'Why not?'

'You'll get me into trouble.'

'Then it must be true.'

Dukhi threw up his hands in mock despair and started collecting his implements.

'It's true, it's true!' I cried, dancing round him, and then I ran indoors to Ayah and said, 'Ayah, Dukhi was in love with the Rani!'

Ayah gave a shriek of laughter, then looked very serious and put her finger against my lips.

'Don't say such things,' she said. 'Dukhi is of a very low caste. People won't like it if they hear what you say. And besides, the Rani told you her prince died and turned into a snake. Well, Dukhi hasn't become a snake as yet, has he?'

True, Dukhi didn't look as though he could be anything but a gardener; but I wasn't satisfied with his denials or with Ayah's attempts to still my tongue. Hadn't Dukhi sent the Rani a nosegay? . . .

A few days before we left, I went to say goodbye to the Rani.

'I'm going away,' I said.

'How lovely!' said the Rani. 'I wish I could go away!'

'Why don't you?'

'They won't let me. They're afraid to let me out

of the palace.'

'What are they afraid of, Your Highness?'

'That I might run away. Run away, far far away, to the land where the leopards are learning to pray.'

Gosh, I thought, she's really quite crazy . . . But then she was silent, and started smoking a small hookah.

She drew on the hookah, looked at me, and asked, 'Where is your mother?'

'I haven't one.'

'Everyone has a mother. Did yours die?'

'No. She went away.'

She drew on her hookah again and then said, very sweetly, 'Don't go away . . .'

'I must,' I said. 'It's because of the war.'

'What war? Is there a war on? You see, no one tells me anything.'

'It's between us and Hitler,' I said.

'And who is Hitler?'

'He's a German.'

'I knew a German once, Dr Schreinherr, he had beautiful hands.'

'Was he an artist?'

'He was a dentist.'

The Rani got up from her couch and

accompanied me out on to the balcony. When we looked down at the garden, we could see Dukhi weeding a flower bed. Both of us gazed down at him in silence, and I wondered what the Rani would say if I asked her if she had ever been in love with the palace gardener. Ayah had told me it would be an insulting question, so I held my peace. But as I walked slowly down the spiral staircase, the Rani's voice came after me.

'Thank him,' she said. 'Thank him for the beautiful rose.'

# My Father and I

The two years I spent with my father were probably the happiest of my childhood—although, for him, they must have been a period of trial and tribulation. Frequent bouts of malaria had undermined his constitution; the separation from my mother weighed heavily on him, and it could not be reversed; and at the age of eight I was self-willed and demanding.

He did his best for me, dear man. He gave me his time, his companionship, his complete attention.

A year was to pass before I was readmitted to a boarding school, and I would have been quite happy never to have gone to school again. My year in the convent had been sufficient punishment for uncommitted sins. I felt that I had earned a year's holiday.

This was in 1943, during World War II. The real war was being fought in Burma and the Far East, but Delhi was full of men in uniform. It was a glorious year, during which we changed our residence at least four times—from a tent on a flat treeless plain outside Delhi, to a hutment near Humayun's tomb; to a couple of rooms on Atul

Grove Road; to a small flat on Hailey Road and, finally, to an apartment in Scindia House, facing the Connaught Circus.

We were not very long in the tent and hutment—but long enough for me to remember the scorching winds of June, and the bhisti's hourly visit to douse the khas-khas matting with water. This turned a hot breeze into a refreshing, fragrant zephyr—for about half an hour. And then the dust and the prickly heat took over again. A small table fan was the only luxury.

Except for Sundays, I was alone during most of the day; my father's office in Air Headquarters was somewhere near India Gate. He'd return at about six, tired but happy to find me in good spirits. For although I had no friends during that period, I found plenty to keep me occupied—my father's books, stamps, the old gramophone, hundreds of postcards which he'd collected during his years in England, a scrapbook, albums of photographs . . . And sometimes I'd explore the jungle behind the tents.

I would have my lunch with a family living in a neighbouring tent, but at night my father and I would eat together. I forget who did the cooking.

But Father made the breakfast himself, getting up early to whip up some fresh butter (he loved doing this) and then laying the table with cornflakes or grapenuts, and eggs poached or fried.

The gramophone was a great companion when my father was away. He had kept all the records he had collected in Jamnagar, and these were added to from time to time. There were operatic arias and duets from *La Bohème* and *Madame Butterfly;* ballads and traditional airs rendered by Paul Robeson, Peter Dawson, Richard Crooks, Webster Booth, Nelson Eddy and other tenors and baritones, and of course the great Russian bass, Chaliapin. And there were lighter, music-hall songs and comic relief provided by Gracie Fields (the 'Lancashire Lass'), George Formby with his ukelele, Arthur Askey, Flanagan and Allan, and a host of other recording artistes.

After a few torrid months in the tent-house and then in a brick hutment, which was even hotter, my father was permitted to rent rooms of his own on Atul Grove Road, a tree-lined lane not far from Connaught Place, which was then the hub and business centre of New Delhi. Keeping me with him had been quite unofficial; his superiors were always wanting to know why my mother wasn't around to look after me. He was really hoping that the war would end soon, so that he could take me to England and put me in a good school there. He had been selling some of his more valuable stamps and had put quite a bit in the bank.

One evening he came home with a bottle of Scotch whisky. This was most unusual, because I had never seen him drinking—not even beer. Had he suddenly decided to hit the bottle? The mystery was solved when an American officer dropped in to have dinner with us (having a guest for dinner was a very rare event). Our guest polished off several pegs of whisky (my father had a drink too), and after dinner, they sat down to go through some of my father's stamp albums. The American collector bought several stamps, and we went to bed richer by a couple of thousand rupees.

That it was possible to make money out of one's hobby was something I was to remember when writing became my passion.

When winter came, my father's khakis were changed for dark blue RAF caps and uniforms, which suited him nicely. He was a good-looking man, always neatly dressed; on the short side but

quite sturdy. He was over forty when he had joined
up—hence the office job, deciphering (or helping to
create) codes and ciphers. He was quite secretive
about it all (as indeed he was supposed to be), and as
he confided in me on almost every subject but his
work, he was obviously a reliable Intelligence
officer.

He did not have many friends in Delhi. There
was the occasional visit to Uncle Fred near the
railway station, and sometimes he'd spend a half
hour with Mr Rankin, who owned a large drapery
shop at Connaught Circus, where officers' uniforms
were tailored. Mr Rankin was another enthusiastic
stamp collector, and the two of them would get
together in Mr Rankin's back office and exchange
stamps or discuss new issues.

Some Sundays, my father and I explored old
tombs and monuments, but going to the pictures
was what we did most. Connaught Place was well
served with cinemas—the Regal, Rivoli, Odeon and
Plaza, all very new and shiny—and they exhibited
the latest Hollywood and British productions. It
was in these cinemas that I discovered the beautiful
Sonja Henie; making love on skates and even getting
married on ice; Nelson and Jeanette making love in

duets; Errol Flynn making love on the high seas; and
Gary Cooper and Claudette Colbert making love in
the bedroom.

When my father broached the subject of sending me
to a boarding school, I used every argument I could
think of to dissuade him. The convent school was
still fresh in my memory and I had no wish to return
to any institution remotely resembling it—certainly
not after almost a year of untrammelled freedom
and my father's companionship.

'Why do you want to send me to school again?' I
asked. 'I can learn more at home. I can read books, I
can write letters, I can even do sums!'

'Not bad for a boy of nine,' said my father. 'But I
can't teach you algebra, physics and chemistry.'

'I don't want to be a chemist.'

'Well, what would you like to be when you grow
up?'

'A tap-dancer.'

'We've been seeing too many pictures. Everyone
says I spoil you.'

I tried another argument. 'You'll have to live on
your own again. You'll feel lonely.'

'That can't be helped, son. But I'll come to see

you as often as I can. You see, they're posting me to Karachi for some time, and then I'll be moved again—they won't allow me to keep you with me at some of these places. Would you like to stay with your mother?'

I shook my head.

'With Calcutta Granny?'

'I don't know her.'

'When the War's over, I'll take you with me to England. But for the next year or two we must stay here. I've found a nice school for you.'

'Another convent?'

'No, it's a prep school for boys in Simla. And I may be able to get posted there during the summer.'

'I want to see it first,' I said.

'We'll go up to Simla together. Not now—in April or May, before it gets too hot. It doesn't matter if you join school a bit later—I know you'll soon catch up with the others.'

There was a brief trip to Dehra Dun. I think my father felt that there was still a chance of a reconciliation with my mother. But her affair with the businessman was far gone. His own wife had been practically abandoned and left to look after the photography shop she'd brought along with her dowry. She was a stout lady with high blood pressure, who once went in search of my mother and stepfather with an axe. Fortunately, they were not at home that day and she had to vent her fury on the furniture.

In later years, when I got to know her quite well, she told me that my father was a very decent man, who treated her with great courtesy and kindness on the occasion they met.

I remember we stayed in a little hotel or boarding house just off the Eastern Canal Road.

Dehra was a green and leafy place. The houses were separated by hedges, not walls, and the residential areas were criss-crossed by little lanes bordered by hibiscus or oleander shrubs.

We were soon back in Delhi.

My parents' separation was final and it was to be almost two years before I saw my mother again.

1944. The war dragged on. No sooner was I back in prep school than my father was transferred to Calcutta. In some ways this was a good thing because my sister Elllen was there, living with 'Calcutta Granny,' and my father could live in his own home for a change. Granny had been living on

Park Lane ever since Grandfather had died.

It meant, of course, that my father couldn't come to see me in Simla during my mid-term holidays. But he wrote regularly—once a week, on an average.

The War was coming to an end, peace was in the air, but there was also talk of the British leaving India as soon as the war was over. In his letters my father spoke of the preparations he was making towards that end. Obviously, he saw no future for us in a free India. He was not an advocate of the Empire but he took a pragmatic approach to the problems of the day.

There would be a new school for me in England, he said, and meanwhile he was selling off large segments of his stamp collection so that we'd have some money to start life afresh when he left the RAF.

My father's last letter to me was the only one that I was able to retain (apart from some of the postcards). It is a good example of the sort of letters he wrote to me, and you can see why I hung on to it.

*AA Bond 108485 (RAF)*
*c/o 231 Group*
*Rafpost*
*Calcutta 20/8/44*

*My dear Ruskin,*

*Thank you very much for your letter received a few days ago. I was pleased to hear that you were quite well and learning hard. We are all quite okay here, but I am still not strong enough to go to work after the recent attack of malaria I had. I was in hospital for a long time and that is the reason why you did not get a letter from me for several weeks.*

*I have now to wear glasses for reading, but I do not use them for ordinary wear—but only when I read or do book work. Ellen does not wear glasses at all now.*

*Do you need any new warm clothes? Your warm suits must be getting too small. I am glad to hear the rains are practically over in the hills where you are. It will be nice to have sunny days in September when your holidays are on. Do the holidays begin from the 9th of Sept? What will you do? Is there to be a Scouts Camp at Taradevi? Or will you catch butterflies on sunny days on the school Cricket*

*Ground? I am glad to hear you have lots of friends. Next year you will be in the top class of the Prep. School. You only have 3½ months more for the Xmas holidays to come round, when you will be glad to come home, I am sure, to do more Stamp work and Library Study. The New Market is full of bookshops here. Ellen loves the market.*

*I wanted to write before about your writing Ruskin, but forgot. Sometimes I get letters from you written in very small handwriting, as if you wanted to squeeze a lot of news into one sheet of letter paper. It is not good for you or for your eyes, to get into the habit of writing small: I know your handwriting is good and that you came 1st in class for handwriting, but try and form a larger style of writing and do not worry if you can't get all your news into one sheet of paper—but stick to big letters.*

*We have had a very wet month just passed. It is still cloudy, at night we have to use fans, but during the cold weather it is nice—not too cold like Delhi and not too warm either—but just moderate. Granny is quite well. She and Ellen send you their fond love. The last I heard a week ago, that William and all at Dehra were well also.*

We have been without a cook for the past few days. I hope we find a good one before long. There are not many. I wish I could get our Delhi cook, the old man now famous for his 'Black Puddings' which Ellen hasn't seen since we arrived in Calcutta 4 months ago.

I have still got the Records and Gramophone and most of the best books, but as they are all getting old and some not suited to you which are only for children under 8 years old—I will give some to William, and Ellen and you can buy some new ones when you come home for Xmas. I am re-arranging all the stamps that became loose and topsy-turvy after people came and went through the collections to buy stamps. A good many got sold, the rest got mixed up a bit and it is now taking up all my time putting the balance of the collection in order. But as I am at home all day, unable to go to work as yet, I have lots of time to finish the work of re-arranging the Collection. Ellen loves drawing. I give her paper and a pencil and let her draw for herself without any help, to get her used to holding paper and pencil. She has got expert at using her pencil now and draws some wonderful animals like camels,     elephants,     dragons     with     many *heads—cobras—rain clouds shedding buckets of water—tigers with long grass around them—horses with manes and wolves and foxes with bushy hair. Sometimes you can't see much of the animals because there is too much grass covering them or too much hair on the foxes and wolves and too much mane on the horses' necks—or too much rain from the clouds. All this decoration is made up by a sort of heavy scribbling of lines, but through it all one can see some very good shapes of animals, elephants and ostriches and other things. I will send you some.*

*Well, Ruskin, I hope this finds you well. With fond love from us all. Write again soon, Ever your loving daddy . . .*

It was about two weeks after receiving this letter that I was given the news of my father's death. Those frequent bouts of malaria had undermined his health, and a severe attack of jaundice did the rest. A kind but inept teacher, Mr Murtough, was given the unenviable task of breaking the news to me. He mumbled something about God needing my father more than I did, and of course I knew what had happened and broke down and had to be taken to the infirmary, where I remained for a couple of days. It never made any sense to me why God should have needed my father more than I did, unless of course He envied my father's stamp collection. If God was Love, why did He have to break up the only loving relationship I'd known so far? What would happen to me now, I wondered . . . would I live with Calcutta Granny or some other relative or be put away in an orphanage?

The headmaster, Mr Priestley, saw me in his office and said I'd be going to my mother when school closed. He said he'd been told that I had kept my father's letters and that if I wished to put them in his safe keeping, he'd see that they were not lost. I handed them over—all except the one I've reproduced here.

The day before we broke up for the school holidays, I went to Mr Priestley and asked for my letters. 'What letters?' He looked bemused, irritated. He'd had a trying day. 'My father's letters,' I told him. 'You said you'd keep them for me.' 'Did I? Don't remember. Why should I want to keep your father's letters?' 'I don't know, sir. You put them in your drawer.' He opened the drawer, shut it. 'None of your letters here. I'm very busy now, Bond. If I find any of your letters, I'll give them to you.' I was dismissed from his presence.

I never saw those letters again. And I'm glad to say I did not see Mr Priestley again.

# My Mother

I'd had this old and faded negative with me for a number of years and had never bothered to make a print from it. It was a picture of my maternal grandparents. I remembered my grandmother quite well, because a large part of my childhood had been spent in her house in Dehra after she had been widowed; but although everyone said she was fond of me, I remembered her as a stern, somewhat aloof person, of whom I was a little afraid.

I hadn't kept many family pictures and this negative was yellow and spotted with damp.

Then last week, when I was visiting my mother in hospital in Delhi, while she awaited her operation, we got talking about my grandparents, and I remembered the negative and decided I'd make a print for my mother.

When I got the photograph and saw my grandmother's face for the first time in twenty-five years, I was immediately struck by my resemblance to her. I have, like her, lived a rather spartan life, happy with my one room, just as she was content to

Extract from *The Last Time I Saw Delhi*

live in a room of her own while the rest of the family took over the house! And like her, I have lived tidily. But I did not know the physical resemblance was so close—the fair hair, the heavy build, the wide forehead. She looks more like me than my mother!

In the photograph she is seated on her favourite chair, at the top of the veranda steps, and Grandfather stands behind her in the shadows thrown by a large mango tree which is not in the picture. I can tell it was a mango tree because of the pattern the leaves make on the wall. Grandfather was a slim, trim man, with a drooping moustache that was fashionable in the twenties. By all accounts he had a mischievous sense of humour, although he looks unwell in the picture. He appears to have been quite swarthy. No wonder he was so successful in dressing up 'native' style and passing himself off as a street-vendor. My mother tells me he even took my grandmother in on one occasion, and sold her a basketful of bad oranges. His character was in strong contrast to my grandmother's rather forbidding personality and Victorian sense of propriety; but they made a god match. Unlike my parents . . .

But here's the picture, and I am taking it to show

it to my mother who lies in Lady Hardinge Hospital, awaiting the removal of her left breast.

It is early August and the day is hot and sultry. It rained during the night, but now the sun is out and the sweat oozes through my shirt as I sit in the back of a stuffy little taxi taking me through the suburbs of Greater New Delhi.

On either side of the road are the houses of well-to-do Punjabis. Industrious, flashy, go-ahead people. Thirty years ago, fields extended on either side of this road, as far as the eye could see. The Ridge, an outcrop of the Aravallis, was scrub jungle, in which the black buck roamed. Feroz Shah's fourteenth-century hunting lodge stood here in splendid isolation. It is still here, hidden by petrol pumps and lost within the sounds of buses, cars, trucks and scooter-rickshaws. The peacock has fled the forest, the black buck is extinct. Only the jackal remains. When, a thousand years from now, the last human has left this contaminated planet for some other star, the jackal and the crow will remain, to survive for years on all the refuse we leave behind.

It is difficult to find the right entrance to the hospital, because for about a mile along the Panchkuin Road the pavement has been obliterated by tea shops, furniture shops and piles of accumulated junk. A public hydrant stands near the gate, and dirty water runs across the road.

I find my mother in a small ward. It is a cool, dark room, and a ceiling fan whirrs pleasantly overhead. A nurse, a dark pretty girl from the south, is attending to my mother. She says, 'In a minute,' and proceeds to make an entry on a chart.

My mother gives me a wan smile and beckons me to come nearer. Her cheeks are slightly flushed, due possibly to fever; otherwise she looks her normal self. I find it hard to believe that the operation she will have tomorrow will only give her, at the most, another year's lease on life.

I sit at the foot of her bed. This is my third visit since I flew back from Jersey, using up all my savings in the process; and I will leave after the operation, not to fly away again, but to return to the hills which have always called me back.

'How do you feel?' I ask.

'All right. They say they will operate in the morning. They've stopped my smoking.'

'Can you drink? Your rum, I mean?'

'No. Not until a few days after the operation.'

She has a fair amount of grey in her hair, natural

enough at fifty-four. Otherwise she hasn't changed much; the same small chin and mouth, lively brown eyes. Her father's face, not her mother's.

The nurse has left us. I produce the photograph and hand it to my mother.

'The negative was lying with me all these years. I had it printed yesterday.'

'I can't see without my glasses.'

The glasses are lying on the locker near her bed. I hand them to her. She puts them on and studies the photograph.

'Your grandmother was always very fond of you.'

'It was hard to tell. She wasn't a soft woman.'

'It was her money that got you to Jersey, when you finished school. It wasn't much, just enough for the ticket.'

'I didn't know that.'

'The only person who ever left you anything. I'm afraid I've nothing to leave you, either.'

'You know very well that I've never cared a damn about money. My father taught me to write. That was inheritance enough.'

'And what did I teach you?'

'I'm not sure . . . Perhaps you taught me how to

enjoy myself now and then.'

She looked pleased at this. 'Yes, I've enjoyed myself between troubles. But your father didn't know how to enjoy himself. That's why we quarrelled so much.'

'He was much older than you.'

'You've always blamed me for leaving him, haven't you?

'I was very small at the time. You left us suddenly. My father had to look after me, and it wasn't easy for him. He was very sick. Naturally, I blamed you.'

'He wouldn't let me take you away.'

'Because you were going to marry someone else.'

I break off; we have been over this before. I am not there as my father's advocate, and the time for recrimination has passed.

And now it is raining outside, and the scent of wet earth comes through the open doors, overpowering the odour of medicines and disinfectants. The dark-eyed nurse comes in again and informs me that the doctor will soon be on his rounds. I can come again in the evening, or early morning before the operation.

'Come in the evening,' says my mother. 'The

others will be here then.'

'I haven't come to see the others.'

'They are looking forward to seeing you.' 'They' being my stepfather and half-brothers.

'I'll be seeing them in the morning.'

'As you like . . .'

And then I am on the road again, standing on the pavement, on the fringe of a chaotic rush of traffic, in which it appears that every vehicle is doing its best to overtake its neighbour. The blare of horns can be heard in the corridors of the hospital, but everyone is conditioned to the noise and pays no attention to it. Rather, the sick and the dying are heartened by the thought that people are still well enough to feel reckless, indifferent to each other's safety! In Delhi there is a feverish desire to be first in line, the first to get anything . . . This is probably because no one ever gets around to dealing with second-comers.

When I hail a scooter-rickshaw and it stops a short distance away, someone elbows his way past me and gets in first.

So I stand on the pavement waiting for another scooter, which doesn't come. In Delhi, to be second in the race is to be last.

I walk all the way back to my small hotel, with a foreboding of having seen my mother for the last time.

# Uncle Ken

## Granny's fabulous kitchen

As kitchens went, it wasn't all that big. It wasn't as big as the bedroom or the living room, but it was big enough, and there was a pantry next to it. What made it fabulous was all that came out of it: good things to eat like cakes and curries, chocolate fudge and peanut toffee, jellies and jam tarts, meat pies, stuffed turkeys, stuffed chickens, stuffed eggplants, and hams stuffed with stuffed chickens.

As far as I was concerned, Granny was the best cook in the whole wide world.

Two generations of Clerkes had lived in India and my maternal grandmother had settled in a small town called Dehra Dun . . .

Granny was glad to have me because she lived alone most of the time. Not entirely alone, though . . . There was a gardener, who lived in an outhouse. And he had a son called Mohan, who was about my age. And there was Ayah, an elderly maidservant, who helped with the household work. And there was a Siamese cat with bright blue eyes, and a mongrel dog called Crazy because he ran circles round the house.

And, of course, there was Uncle Ken, Granny's nephew, who came to stay whenever he was out of a job (which was quite often) or when he felt like enjoying some of Granny's cooking.

Roast Duck. This was one of Granny's specials. The first time I had roast duck at Granny's place, Uncle Ken was there too.

He'd just lost a job as a railway guard, and had come to stay with Granny until he could find another job. He always stayed as long as he could, only moving on when Granny offered to get him a job as an assistant master in Padre Lai's Academy for Small Boys. Uncle Ken couldn't stand small boys. They made him nervous, he said. I made him nervous too, but there was only one of me, and there was always Granny to protect him. At Padre Lal's, there were over a hundred small boys.

Although Uncle Ken had a tremendous appetite, and ate just as much as I did, he never praised Granny's dishes. I think this is why I was annoyed with him at times, and why sometimes I enjoyed making him feel nervous.

Uncle Ken looked down at the roast duck, his glasses slipping down to the edge of his nose.

'Hm . . . Duck again, Aunt Ellen?'

'What do you mean, duck again? You haven't had duck since you were here last month.'

'That's what I mean,' said Uncle Ken. 'Somehow, one expects more variety from you, Aunt.'

All the same, he took two large helpings and ate most of the stuffing before I could get at it. I took my revenge by emptying all the apple sauce onto my plate. Uncle Ken knew I loved the stuffing; and I knew he was crazy about Granny's apple sauce. So we were even.

'When are you joining your parents?' he asked hopefully, over the jam tart.

'I may not go to them this year,' I said. 'When are you getting another job, Uncle?'

'Oh, I'm thinking of taking a rest for a couple of months.'

I enjoyed helping Granny and Ayah with the washing up. While we were at work, Uncle Ken would take a siesta on the veranda or switch on the radio to listen to dance music. Glenn Miller and his Swing Band was all the rage then.

'And how do you like your Uncle Ken?' asked Granny one day, as she emptied the bones from his plate into the dog's bowl.

'I wish he was someone else's Uncle,' I said.

'He's not so bad, really. Just eccentric.'

'What's eccentric?'

'Oh, just a little crazy.'

'At least Crazy runs round the house,' I said. 'I've never seen Uncle Ken running.'

But I did one day.

Mohan and I were playing marbles in the shade of the mango grove when we were taken aback by the sight of Uncle Ken charging across the compound, pursued by a swarm of bees. He'd been smoking a cigar under a silk-cotton tree, and the fumes had disturbed the wild bees in their hive, directly above him. Uncle Ken fled indoors and leapt into a tub of cold water. He had received a few stings and decided to remain in bed for three days. Ayah took his meals to him on a tray.

'I didn't know Uncle Ken could run so fast,' I said, later that day.

'It's nature's way of compensating,' said Granny.

'What's compensating?'

'Making up for things . . . Now at least Uncle Ken knows that he can run. Isn't that wonderful?' . . .

'It's high time you found a job,' said Granny to Uncle Ken one day.

'There are no jobs in Dehra,' complained Uncle Ken.

'How can you tell? You've never looked for one. And anyway, you don't have to stay here for ever. Your sister Emily is headmistress of a school in Lucknow. You could go to her. She said before that she was ready to put you in charge of a dormitory.'

'Bah!' said Uncle Ken. 'Honestly, Aunt, you don't expect me to look after a dormitory seething with forty or fifty demented small boys?'

'What's demented?' I asked.

'Shut up,' said Uncle Ken.

'It means crazy,' said Granny.

'So many words mean crazy,' I complained. 'Why don't we just say crazy. We have a crazy dog, and now Uncle Ken is crazy too.'

Uncle Ken clipped me over my ear, and Granny said, 'Your Uncle isn't crazy, so don't be disrespectful. He's just lazy.'

'And eccentric,' I said. 'I heard he was eccentric.'

'Who said I was eccentric?' demanded Uncle Ken.

'Miss Leslie,' I lied. I knew Uncle Ken was fond of Miss Leslie, who ran a beauty parlour in Dehra's smart shopping centre, Astley Hall.

'I don't believe you,' said Uncle Ken. 'Anyway, when did you see Miss Leslie?'

'We sold her a bottle of mint chutney last week. I told her you liked mint chutney. But she said she'd bought it for Mr Brown who's taking her to the pictures tomorrow.'

## Uncle Ken does nothing

To our surprise, Uncle Ken got a part-time job as a guide, showing tourists the 'sights' around Dehra.

There was an old fort near the river bed; and a seventeenth-century temple; and a jail where Pandit Nehru had spent some time as a political prisoner; and, about ten miles into the foothills, the hot sulphur springs.

Uncle Ken told us he was taking a party of six American tourists, husbands and wives, to the sulphur springs. Granny was pleased. Uncle Ken was busy at last! She gave him a hamper filled with ham sandwiches, home-made biscuits and a dozen oranges—ample provision for a day's outing.

The sulphur springs were only ten miles from Dehra, but we didn't see Uncle Ken for three days.

He was a sight when he got back. His clothes were dusty and torn; his cheeks were sunken; and the little bald patch on top of his head had been burnt a bright red.

'What have you been doing to yourself?' asked Granny.

Uncle Ken sank into the armchair on the veranda. 'I'm starving, Aunt Ellen. Give me something to eat.'

'What happened to the food you took with you?'

'There were seven of us, and it was all finished on the first day.'

'Well, it was only supposed to last a day. You said you were going to the sulphur springs.'

'Yes, that's where we were going,' said Uncle Ken. 'But we never reached them. We got lost in the hills.'

'How could you possibly have got lost in the hills? You had only to walk straight along the river bed and up the valley . . . You ought to know, you were the guide and you'd been there before, when my husband was alive.'

'Yes, I know,' said Uncle Ken, looking crestfallen. 'But I forgot the way. That is, I forgot the valley. I mean, I took them up the wrong valley. And I kept thinking the springs would be at the same river, but it wasn't the same river . . . So we kept walking, until we were in the hills, and then I looked down and saw we'd come up the wrong valley. We had to spend the night under the stars. It was very, very cold. And next day I thought we'd come back a quicker way, through Mussoorie, but we took the wrong path and reached Kempti instead . . . And then we walked down to the motor road and caught a bus.'

I helped Granny put Uncle Ken to bed, and then I helped her make him a strengthening onion soup. I took him the soup on a tray, and he made a face while drinking it and then asked for more. He was in bed for two days, while Ayah and I took turns taking him his meals. He wasn't a bit graceful.

When Uncle Ken complained he was losing his hair and that his bald patch was increasing in size,

Granny looked up her book of old recipes and said there was one for baldness which Grandfather had used with great success. It consisted of a lotion made with gherkins soaked in brandy. Uncle Ken said he'd try it.

Granny soaked some gherkins in brandy for a week, then gave the bottle to Uncle Ken with instructions to rub a little into his scalp mornings and evenings.

Next day, when she looked into his room, she found only gherkins in the bottle. Uncle Ken had drunk all the brandy.

Uncle Ken liked to whistle.

Hands in his pockets, nothing to do, he would stroll about the house, around the garden, up and down the road, whistling feebly to himself.

It was always the same whistle, tuneless to everyone except my uncle.

'What are you whistling today, Uncle Ken?' I'd ask.

" 'Ol' Man River". Don't you recognize it?'

And the next time around he'd be whistling the same notes, and I'd say, 'Still whistling "Ol' Man River", Uncle?'

'No, I'm not. This is "Danny Boy". Can't you tell the difference?'

And he'd slouch off, whistling tunelessly.

Sometimes it irritated Granny.

'Can't you stop whistling, Ken? It gets on my nerves. Why don't you try singing for a change?'

'I can't. It's "The Blue Danube", there aren't any words,' and he'd waltz around the kitchen, whistling.

'Well, you can do your whistling and waltzing on the veranda,' Granny would say. 'I won't have it in the kitchen. It spoils the food.'

When Uncle Ken had a bad tooth removed by our dentist, Dr Kapadia, we thought his whistling would stop. But it only became louder and shriller.

One day, while he was strolling along the road, hands in his pockets, doing nothing, whistling very loudly, a girl on a bicycle passed him. She stopped suddenly, got off the bicycle, and blocked his way.

'If you whistle at me every time I pass, Kenneth Clerke,' she said, 'I'll wallop you!'

Uncle Ken went red in the face. 'I wasn't whistling at you,' he said.

'Well, I don't see anyone else on the road.'

'I was whistling "God Save The King". Don't

you recognize it?'

## Uncle Ken on the job

'We'll have to do something about Uncle Ken,' said Granny to the world at large.

I was in the kitchen with her, shelling peas and popping a few into my mouth now and then. Suzie, the Siamese cat, sat on the sideboard, patiently watching Granny prepare an Irish stew. Suzie liked Irish stew.

'It's not that I mind him staying,' said Granny, 'and I don't want any money from him, either. But it isn't healthy for a young man to remain idle for so long.'

'Is Uncle Ken a young man, Gran?'

'He's forty. Everyone says he'll improve as he grows up.'

'He could go and live with Aunt Mabel.'

'He *does* go and live with Aunt Mabel. He also lives with Aunt Emily and Aunt Beryl. That's his trouble—he has too many doting sisters ready to put him up and put up with him . . . Their husbands are all quite well-off and can afford to have him now and then. So our Ken spends three months with Mabel, three months with Beryl, three months with me. That way he gets through the year as everyone's guest and doesn't have to worry about making a living.'

'He's lucky in a way,' I said.

'His luck won't last forever. Already Mabel is talking of going to New Zealand. And once India is free—in just a year or two from now—Emily and Beryl will probably go off to England, because their husbands are in the army and all the British officers will be leaving.'

'Can't Uncle Ken follow them to England?'

'He knows he'll have to start working if he goes there. When your aunts find they have to manage without servants, they won't be ready to keep Ken for long periods. In any case, who's going to pay his fare to England or New Zealand?'

'If he can't go, he'll stay here with you, Granny. You'll be here, won't you?'

'Not forever. Only while I live.'

'You won't go to England?'

'No, I've grown up here. I'm like the trees. I've taken root, I won't be going away—not until, like an old tree, I'm without any more leaves . . . You'll go though, when you are bigger. You'll probably finish your schooling abroad.'

'I'd rather finish it here. I want to spend all my holidays with you. If I go away, who'll look after you when you grow old?'

'I'm old already. Over sixty.'

'Is that very old? It's only a little older than Uncle Ken. And how will you look after him when you're *really* old?'

'He can look after himself if he tries. And it's time he started. It's time he took a job.'

I pondered on the problem. I could think of nothing that would suit Uncle Ken—or rather, I could think of no one who would find him suitable. It was Ayah who made a suggestion.

'The Maharani of Jetpur needs a tutor for her children,' she said. 'Just a boy and a girl.'

'How do you know?' asked Granny.

'I heard it from their ayah. The pay is two hundred rupees a month, and there is not much work—only two hours every morning.'

'That should suit Uncle Ken,' I said.

'Yes, it's a good idea,' said Granny. 'We'll have to talk him into applying. He ought to go over and see them. The Maharani is a good person to work for.'

Uncle Ken agreed to go over and inquire about

the job. The Maharani was out when he called, but he was interviewed by the Maharaja.

'Do you play tennis?' asked the Maharaja.

'Yes,' said Uncle Ken, who remembered having played a bit of tennis when he was a schoolboy.

'In that case, the job's yours. I've been looking for a fourth player for a doubles match . . . By the way, were you at Cambridge?'

'No, I was at Oxford,' said Uncle Ken.

The Maharaja was impressed. An Oxford man who could play tennis was just the sort of tutor he wanted for his children.

When Uncle Ken told Granny about the interview, she said, 'But you haven't been to Oxford, Ken. How could you say that!'

'Of course I have been to Oxford. Don't you remember? I spent two years there with your brother Jim!'

'Yes, but you were helping him in his pub in the town. You weren't at the University.'

'Well, the Maharaja never asked me if I had been to the University. He asked me if I was at Cambridge, and I said no, I was at Oxford, which was perfectly true. He didn't ask me what I was doing at Oxford. What difference does it make?'

And he strolled off, whistling.

To our surprise, Uncle Ken was a great success in his job. In the beginning, anyway.

The Maharaja was such a poor tennis player that he was delighted to discover that there was someone who was even worse. So, instead of becoming a doubles partner for the Maharaja, Uncle Ken became his favourite singles opponent. As long as he could keep losing to His Highness, Uncle Ken's job was safe.

In between tennis matches and accompanying his employer on duck shoots, Uncle Ken squeezed in a few lessons for the children, teaching them reading, writing and arithmetic. Sometimes he took me along, so that I could tell him when he got his sums wrong. Uncle Ken wasn't very good at subtraction, although he could add fairly well.

The Maharaja's children were smaller than me. Uncle Ken would leave me with them, saying, 'Just see that they do their sums properly, Ruskin,' and he would stroll off to the tennis courts, hands in his pockets, whistling tunelessly

Even if his pupils had different answers to the same sum, he would give both of them an encouraging pat, saying, 'Excellent, excellent. I'm glad to see both of you trying so hard. One of you is right and one of you is wrong, but as I don't want to discourage either of you, I won't say who's right and who's wrong!'

But afterwards, on the way home, he'd ask me, 'Which was the right answer, Ruskin?'

Uncle Ken always maintained that he would never have lost his job if he hadn't beaten the Maharaja at tennis.

Not that Uncle Ken had any intention of winning. But by playing occasional games with the Maharaja's secretaries and guests, his tennis had improved and so, try as hard as he might to lose, he couldn't help winning a match against his employer.

The Maharaja was furious.

'Mr Clerke,' he said sternly, 'I don't think you realize the importance of losing. We can't all win, you know. Where would the world be without losers?'

'I'm terribly sorry,' said Uncle Ken. 'It was just a fluke, your Highness.'

The Maharaja accepted Uncle Ken's apologies; but a week later it happened again. Kenneth Clerke won and the Maharaja stormed off the court without saying a word. The following day he turned up at lesson time. As usual Uncle Ken and the children were engaged in a game of noughts and crosses.

'We won't be requiring your services from tomorrow, Mr Clerke. I've asked my secretary to give you a month's salary in lieu of notice.'

Uncle Ken came home with his hands in his pockets, whistling cheerfully.

'You're early,' said Granny.

'They don't need me any more,' said Uncle Ken.

'Oh well, never mind. Come in and have your tea.' Granny must have known the job wouldn't last very long. And she wasn't one to nag. As she said later, 'At least he tried. And it lasted longer than most of his jobs—two months.'

## Uncle Ken at the wheel

On my next visit to Dehra, Mohan met me at the station. We got into a tonga with my luggage and we went rattling and jingling along Dehra's quiet roads to Granny's house.

'Tell me all the news, Mohan.'

'Not much to tell. Some of the sahibs are selling

their houses and going away. Suzie has had kittens.'

Granny knew I'd been in the train for two nights, and she had a huge breakfast ready for me. Porridge, scrambled eggs on toast. Bacon with fried tomatoes. Toast and marmalade. Sweet milky tea.

She told me there'd been a letter from Uncle Ken.

'He says he's the assistant manager in Firpo's hotel in Simla,' she said. 'The salary is very good, and he gets free board and lodging. It's a steady job and I hope he keeps it.'

Three days later Uncle Ken was on the veranda steps with his bedding roll and battered suitcase.

'Have you given up the hotel job?' asked Granny.

'No,' said Uncle Ken. 'They have closed down.'

'I hope it wasn't because of you.'

'No, Aunt Ellen. The bigger hotels in the hill stations are all closing down.'

'Well, never mind. Come along and have your tiffin. There is a kofta curry today. It's Ruskin's favourite.'

'Oh, is he here too? I have far too many nephews and nieces. Still he's preferable to those two girls of Mabel's. They made life miserable for me all the time I was with them in Simla.'

Over tiffin (as lunch was called in those days), Uncle Ken talked very seriously about ways and means of earning a living.

'There is only one taxi in the whole of Dehra,' he mused. 'Surely there is business for another?'

'I'm sure there is,' said Granny. 'But where does it get you? In the first place, you don't have a taxi. And in the second place, you can't drive.'

'I can soon learn. There's a driving school in town. And I can use Uncle's old car. It's been gathering dust in the garage for years.' (He was referring to Grandfather's vintage Hillman Roadster. It was a 1926 model: about twenty years old.)

'I don't think it will run now,' said Granny.

'Of course it will. It just needs some oiling and greasing and a spot of paint.'

'All right, learn to drive. Then we will see about the Roadster.'

So Uncle Ken joined the driving school.

He was very regular, going for his lessons for an hour in the evening. Granny paid the fee.

After a month Uncle Ken announced that he

---

In the early 1940s Dehra had only one or two taxis. Today, there are over 500 plying in the town.

could drive and that he was taking the Roadster out for a trial run.

'You haven't got your licence yet,' said Granny.

'Oh, I won't take her far,' said Uncle Ken. 'Just down the road and back again.'

He spent all morning cleaning up the car. Granny gave him money for a can of petrol.

After tea, Uncle Ken said, 'Come along, Ruskin, hop in and I will give you a ride. Bring Mohan along too.' Mohan and I needed no urging. We got into the car beside Uncle Ken.

'Now don't go too fast, Ken,' said Granny anxiously. 'You are not used to the car as yet.'

Uncle Ken nodded and smiled and gave two sharp toots on the horn. He was feeling pleased with himself.

Driving through the gate, he nearly ran over Crazy.

Miss Kellner, coming out for her evening rickshaw ride, saw Uncle Ken at the wheel of the Roadster and went indoors again.

Uncle Ken drove straight and fast, tootling the horn without a break.

At the end of the road there was a roundabout.

'We'll turn here,' said Uncle Ken, 'and then drive

back again.'

He turned the steering wheel; we began going round the roundabout; but the steering wheel wouldn't turn all the way, not as much as Uncle Ken would have liked it to . . . So, instead of going round, we took a right turn and kept going, straight on—and straight through the Maharaja of Jetpur's garden wall.

It was a single-brick wall, and the Roadster knocked it down and emerged on the other side without any damage to the car or any of its occupants. Uncle Ken brought it to a halt in the middle of the Maharaja's lawn.

Running across the grass came the Maharaja himself, flanked by his secretaries and their assistants. When he saw that it was Uncle Ken at the wheel, the Maharaja beamed with pleasure.

'Delighted to see you, old chap!' he exclaimed. 'Jolly decent of you to drop in again. How about a game of tennis?'

## Uncle Ken at the wicket

Although restored to the Maharaja's favour, Uncle Ken was still without a job.

Granny refused to let him take the Hillman out

again and so he decided to sulk. He said it was all Grandfather's fault for not seeing to the steering wheel ten years ago, while he was still alive. Uncle Ken went on a hunger strike for two hours (between tiffin and tea), and we did not hear him whistle for several days.

'The blessedness of silence,' said Granny.

And then he announced that he was going to Lucknow to stay with Aunt Emily.

'She has three children and a school to look after,' said Granny. 'Don't stay too long.'

'She doesn't mind how long I stay,' said Uncle Ken and off he went.

His visit to Lucknow was a memorable one, and we only heard about it much later.

When Uncle Ken got down at Lucknow station, he found himself surrounded by a large crowd, every one waving to him and shouting words of welcome in Hindi, Urdu and English. Before he could make out what it was all about, he was smothered by garlands of marigolds. A young man came forward and announced, 'The Gomti Cricketing Association welcomes you to the historical city of Lucknow,' and promptly led Uncle Ken out of the station to a waiting car.

It was only when the car drove into the sports' stadium that Uncle Ken realized that he was expected to play in a cricket match.

This is what had happened.

Bruce Hallam, the famous English cricketer, was touring India and had agreed to play in a charity match at Lucknow. But the previous evening, in Delhi, Bruce had gone to bed with an upset stomach and hadn't been able to get up in time to catch the train. A telegram was sent to the organizers of the match in Lucknow; but, like many a telegram, it did not reach its destination. The cricket fans of Lucknow had arrived at the station in droves to welcome the great cricketer. And by a strange coincidence, Uncle Ken bore a startling resemblance to Bruce Hallam; even the bald patch on the crown of his head was exactly like Hallam's. Hence the muddle. And, of course, Uncle Ken was always happy to enter into the spirit of a muddle.

Having received from the Gomti Cricketing Association a rousing reception and a magnificent breakfast at the stadium, he felt that it would be very unsporting on his part if he refused to play cricket for them. 'If I can hit a tennis ball,' he mused, 'I ought to be able to hit a cricket ball.' And, luckily, there was a blazer and a pair of white flannels in his suitcase.

The Gomti team won the toss and decided to bat. Uncle Ken was expected to go in at number three, Bruce Hallam's normal position. And he soon found himself walking to the wicket, wondering why on earth no one had as yet invented a more comfortable kind of pad.

The first ball he received was short-pitched, and he was able to deal with it in tennis fashion, swatting it to the mid-wicket boundary. He got no runs, but the crowd cheered.

The next ball took Uncle Ken on the pad. He was right in front of his wicket and should have been given out lbw. But the umpire hesitated to raise his finger. After all, hundreds of people had paid good money to see Bruce Hallam play, and it would have been a shame to disappoint them. 'Not out,' said the umpire.

The third ball took the edge of Uncle Ken's bat and sped through the slips.

'Lovely shot!' exclaimed an elderly gentleman in the pavilion.

'A classic late cut,' said another.

The ball reached the boundary and Uncle Ken

had four runs to his name. Then it was 'Over', and
the other batsman had to face the bowling. He took
a run off the first ball and called for a second run.
Uncle Ken thought one run was more than enough.
Why go charging up and down the wicket like a mad
man? However, he couldn't refuse to run, and he
was halfway down the pitch when the fielder's
throw hit the wicket. Uncle Ken was run-out by
yards. There could be no doubt about it this time.

He returned to the pavilion to the sympathetic
applause of the crowd.

'Not his fault,' said the elderly gentleman. 'The
other chap shouldn't have called. There wasn't a
run there. Still, it was worth coming here all the way
from Kanpur if only to see that superb late cut . . .'

Uncle Ken enjoyed a hearty tiffin-lunch (taken at
noon), and then, realizing that the Gomti team
would probably have to be in the field for most of
the afternoon—more running about!—he slipped
out of the pavilion, left the stadium, and took a
tonga to Aunt Emily's house in the cantonment.

He was just in time for a second lunch (taken at
one o'clock) with Aunt Emily's family: and it was
presumed at the stadium that Bruce Hallam had left

early, to catch the train to Allahabad, where he was expected to play in another charity match.

Aunt Emily, a forceful woman, fed Uncle Ken for a week, and then put him to work in the boys' dormitory of her school. It was several months before he was able to save up enough money to run away and return to Granny's place.

But he had the satisfaction of knowing that he had helped the great Bruce Hallam to add another four runs to his grand aggregate. The scorebook of the Gomti Cricketing Association had recorded his feat for all time:

'B. Hallam run-out 4'

The Gomti team lost the match. But, as Uncle Ken would readily admit, where would we be without losers?

## Bansi and the Ayah

It was a warm spring day in Dehra Dun, and the walls of the bungalow were aflame with flowering bougainvillea. Grandmother sat in an easy chair in a shady corner of the veranda, her knitting needles clicking away, her head nodding now and then.

We heard the jingle of tonga-bells at the gate and a familiar horse-buggy came rattling up the drive. 'I'll see who's come,' I said, and ran down the veranda steps and across the garden.

It was Bansi Lal in his tonga. There were many tongas and tonga drivers in Dehra but Bansi was my favourite driver. He was young and handsome and he always wore a clean white shirt and pyjamas. His pony, too, was bigger and faster than the other tonga ponies.

Bansi didn't have a passenger, so I asked him, 'What have you come for, Bansi?'

'Your grandmother sent for me, dost.' He did not call me 'chhota sahib' or 'baba', but 'dost' and this made me feel much more important. Not every small boy could boast of a tonga driver

Extract from *The Last Tonga Ride*

for his friend!

'Where are you going, Granny?' I asked, after I had run back to the veranda.

'I'm going to the bank.'

'Can I come too?'

'Whatever for? What will you do in the bank?'

'Oh, I won't come inside, I'll sit in the tonga with Bansi.'

'Come along, then.'

We helped Grandmother into the back seat of the tonga, and then I joined Bansi in the driver's seat. He said something to his pony and the pony set off at a brisk trot, out of the gate and down the road.

'Now, not too fast, Bansi,' said Grandmother, who didn't like anything that went too fast—tonga, motor car, train, or bullock cart.

'Fast?' said Bansi. 'Have no fear, memsahib. This pony has never gone fast in its life. Even if a bomb went off behind us, we could go no faster. I have another pony which I use for racing when customers are in a hurry. This pony is reserved for you, memsahib.'

There was no other pony, but Grandmother did not know this, and was mollified by the assurance that she was riding in the slowest tonga in Dehra.

A ten-minute ride brought us to the bazaar. Grandmother's bank, the Allahabad Bank, stood near the Clock Tower. She was gone for about half-an-hour and during this period Bansi and I sauntered about in front of the shops. The pony had been left with some green stuff to munch.

'Do you have any money on you?' asked Bansi.

'Four annas,' I said.

'Just enough for two cups of tea,' said Bansi, putting his arm round my shoulders and guiding me towards a tea stall. The money passed from my palm to his.

'You can have tea, if you like,' I said. 'I'll have a lemonade.'

'So be it, friend. A tea and a lemonade, and be quick about it,' said Bansi to the boy in the tea shop and presently the drinks were set before us and Bansi was making a sound rather like his pony when it drank, while I burped my way through some green, gaseous stuff that tasted more like soap than lemonade.

When Grandmother came out of the bank, she looked pensive and did not talk much during the ride back to the house except to tell me to behave myself when I leant over to pat the pony on its rump.

After paying off Bansi, she marched straight indoors.

'When will you come again?' I asked Bansi.

'When my services are required, dost. I have to make a living, you know. But I tell you what, since we are friends, the next time I am passing this way after leaving a fare, I will jingle my bells at the gate and if you are free and would like a ride—a fast ride!—you can join me. It won't cost you anything. Just bring some money for a cup of tea.'

'All right—since we are friends,' I said.

'Since we are friends.'

And touching the pony very lightly with the handle of his whip, he sent the tonga rattling up the drive and out of the gate. I could hear Bansi singing as the pony cantered down the road.

Ayah was waiting for me in the bedroom, her hands resting on her broad hips—sure sign of an approaching storm.

'So you went off to the bazaar without telling me,' she said. (It wasn't enough that I had Grandmother's permission!) 'And all this time I've been waiting to give you your bath.'

'It's too late now, isn't it?' I asked hopefully.

'No, it isn't. There's still an hour left for lunch.

Off with your clothes!'

While I undressed, Ayah berated me for keeping the company of tonga drivers like Bansi. I think she was a little jealous.

'He is a rogue, that man. He drinks, gambles, and smokes opium. He has TB and other terrible diseases. So don't you be too friendly with him, understand, baba?'

I nodded my head sagely but said nothing. I thought Ayah was exaggerating as she always did about people, and besides, I had no intention of giving up free tonga rides . . .

The clip-clop of a tonga pony, and Bansi's tonga came rattling down the road. I was up in the ancient banyan tree behind the house. I called down to him and he reined in with a shout of surprise, and looked up into the branches of the tree.

'What are you doing up there?' he cried.

'Hiding from Grandmother,' I said.

'And when are you coming for that ride?'

'On Tuesday afternoon,' I said.

'Why not today?'

'Ayah won't let me. But she has Tuesdays off.'

Bansi spat red paan juice across the road. 'Your

ayah is jealous,' he said.

'I know,' I said. 'Women are always jealous, aren't they? I suppose it's because she doesn't have a tonga.'

'It's because she doesn't have a tonga driver,' said Bansi, grinning up at me. 'Never mind. I'll come on Tuesday—that's the day after tomorrow, isn't it?'

I nodded down to him, and then started backing along my branch, because I could hear Ayah calling in the distance. Bansi leant forward and smacked his pony across the rump, and the tonga shot forward.

'What were you doing up there?' asked Ayah a little later.

'I was watching a snake cross the road,' I said. I knew she couldn't resist talking about snakes. There weren't as many in Dehra as there had been in Kathiawar and she was thrilled that I had seen one.

'Was it moving towards you or away from you?' she asked.

'It was going away.'

Ayah's face clouded over. 'That means poverty for the beholder,' she said gloomily.

Later, while scrubbing me down in the bathroom, she began to air all her prejudices, which included drunkards ('they die quickly, anyway'), misers ('they get murdered sooner or later') and tonga drivers ('they have all the vices').

'You are a very lucky boy,' she said suddenly, peering closely at my tummy.

'Why?' I asked. 'You just said I would be poor because I saw a snake going the wrong way.'

'Well, you won't be poor for long. You have a mole on your tummy and that's very lucky. And there is one under your armpit, which means you will be famous. Do you have one on the neck? No, thank God! A mole on the neck is the sign of a murderer!'

'Do you have any moles?' I asked.

Ayah nodded seriously, and pulling her sleeve up to her shoulder, showed me a large mole high on her arm.

'What does that mean?' I asked.

'It means a life of great sadness,' said Ayah gloomily.

'Can I touch it?' I asked.

'Yes, touch it,' she said, and taking my hand, she placed it against the mole.

'It's a nice mole,' I said, wanting to make Ayah happy. 'Can I kiss it?'

'You can kiss it,' said Ayah.

I kissed her on the mole.

'That's nice,' she said.

Tuesday afternoon came at last, and as soon as Grandmother was asleep and Ayah had gone to the bazaar, I was at the gate, looking up and down the road for Bansi and his tonga. He was not long in coming. Before the tonga turned into the road, I could hear his voice, singing to the accompaniment of the carriage bells.

He reached down, took my hand, and hoisted me on to the seat beside him. Then we went off down the road at a steady jog-trot. It was only when we reached the outskirts of the town that Bansi encouraged his pony to greater efforts. He rose in his seat, leaned forward and slapped the pony across the haunches. From a brisk trot we changed to a carefree canter. The tonga swayed from side to side. I clung to Bansi's free arm, while he grinned at me, his mouth red with paan juice.

'Where shall we go, dost?' he asked.

'Nowhere,' I said. 'Anywhere.'

'We'll go to the river,' said Bansi.

The 'river' was really a swift mountain stream

that ran through the forests outside Dehra, joining the Ganga about fifteen miles away. It was almost dry during the winter and early summer; in flood during the monsoon.

The road out of Dehra was a gentle decline and soon we were rushing headlong through the tea gardens and eucalyptus forests, the pony's hoofs striking sparks off the metalled road, the carriage wheels groaning and creaking so loudly that I feared one of them would come off and that we would all be thrown into a ditch or into the small canal that ran beside the road. We swept through mango groves, through guava and litchi orchards, past broad-leaved sal and shisham trees. Once in the sal forest, Bansi turned the tonga on to a rough cart track, and we continued along it for about a furlong, until the road dipped down to the stream bed.

'Let us go straight into the water,' said Bansi. 'You and I and the pony!' And he drove the tonga straight into the middle of the stream, where the water came up to the pony's knees.

'I am not a great one for baths,' said Bansi, 'but the pony needs one, and why should a horse smell sweeter than its owner?' saying which, he flung off his clothes and jumped into the water.

'Better than bathing under a tap!' he cried, slapping himself on the chest and thighs. 'Come down, dost and join me!'

After some hesitation I joined him, but had some difficulty in keeping on my feet in the fast current. I grabbed at the pony's tail and hung on to it, while Bansi began sloshing water over the patient animal's back.

After this, Bansi led both me and the pony out of the stream and together we gave the carriage a good washing down. I'd had a free ride and Bansi got the services of a free helper for the long overdue spring-cleaning of his tonga. After we had finished the job, he presented me with a packet of aam papad—a sticky toffee made from mango pulp—and for some time I tore at it as a dog tears at a bit of old leather. Then I felt drowsy and lay down on the brown, sun-warmed grass. Crickets and grasshoppers were telephoning each other from tree and bush and a pair of bluejays rolled, dived, and swooped acrobatically overhead.

Bansi had no watch. He looked carefully at the sun and said, 'It is past three. When will that ayah of yours be home? She is more frightening than your grandmother!'

'She comes at four.'

'Then we must hurry back. And don't tell her where we've been, or I'll never be able to come to your house again. Your grandmother's one of my best customers.'

'That means you'd be sorry if she died.'

'I would indeed, my friend.'

Bansi raced the tonga back to town. There was very little motor traffic in those days, and tongas and bullock carts were far more numerous than they are today.

We were back five minutes before Ayah returned. Before Bansi left, he promised to take me for another ride the following week.

# Bhabiji and Her Family

(*My neighbours in Rajouri Garden back in the 1960s were the Kamal family. This entry from my journal, which I wrote on one of my later visits, describes a typical day in that household.*)

At first light there is a tremendous burst of birdsong from the guava tree in the little garden. Over a hundred sparrows wake up all at once and give tongue to whatever it is that sparrows have to say to each other at five o'clock on a foggy winter's morning in Delhi.

In the small house, people sleep on; that is, everyone except Bhabiji—Granny—the head of the lively Punjabi middle-class family with whom I nearly always stay when I am in Delhi.

She coughs, stirs, groans, grumbles and gets out of bed. The fire has to be lit, and food prepared for two of her sons to take to work. There is a daughter-in-law, Shobha, to help her; but the girl is not very bright at getting up in the morning. Actually, it is this way: Bhabiji wants to show up her

---

The story originally appeared as *Bhabiji's House*

daughter-in-law; so, no matter how hard Shobha tries to be up first, Bhabiji forestalls her. The old lady does not sleep well, anyway; her eyes are open long before the first sparrow chirps, and as soon as she sees her daughter-in-law stirring, she scrambles out of bed and hurries to the kitchen. This gives her the opportunity to say, 'What good is a daughter-in-law when I have to get up to prepare her husband's food?'

The truth is that Bhabiji does not like anyone else preparing her sons' food.

She looks no older than when I first saw her ten years ago. She still has complete control over a large family and, with tremendous confidence and enthusiasm, presides over the lives of three sons, a daughter, two daughters-in-law and fourteen grandchildren. This is a joint family (there are not many left in a big city like Delhi), in which the sons and their families all live together as one unit under their mother's benevolent (and sometimes slightly malevolent) autocracy. Even when her husband was alive, Bhabiji dominated the household.

The eldest son, Shiv, has a separate kitchen, but his wife and children participate in all the family celebrations and quarrels. It is a small miracle how everyone (including myself when I visit) manages to fit into the house; and a stranger might be forgiven for wondering where everyone sleeps, for no beds are visible during the day. That is because the beds—light wooden frames with rough string across—are brought in only at night, and are taken out first thing in the morning and kept in the garden shed.

As Bhabiji lights the kitchen fire, the household begins to stir, and Shobha joins her mother-in-law in the kitchen. As a guest I am privileged and may get up last. But my bed soon becomes an island battered by waves of scurrying, shouting children, eager to bathe, dress, eat and find their school books. Before I can get up, someone brings me a tumbler of hot sweet tea. It is a brass tumbler and burns my fingers; I have yet to learn how to hold one properly. Punjabis like their tea with lots of milk and sugar—so much so that I often wonder why they bother to add any tea.

Ten years ago, 'bed tea' was unheard of in Bhabiji's house. Then, the first time I came to stay, Kamal, the youngest son, told Bhabiji, 'My friend is *Angrez*. He must have tea in bed.' He forgot to mention that I usually took my morning cup at

seven; they gave it to me at five. I gulped it down and
went to sleep again. Then, slowly, others in the
household began indulging in morning cups of tea.
Now everyone, including the older children, has
'bed tea'. They bless my English forebears for
instituting the custom; I bless the Punjabis for
perpetuating it.

Breakfast is by rota, in the kitchen. It is a tiny
room and accommodates only four adults at a time.
The children have eaten first; but the smallest
children, Shobha's toddlers, keep coming in and
climbing over us. Says Bhabiji of the youngest and
most mischievous, 'He lives only because God keeps
a special eye on him.'

Kamal, his elder brother, Arun, and I sit
cross-legged and barefooted on the floor while
Bhabiji serves us hot parathas stuffed with potatoes
and onions, along with omelettes, an excellent dish.
Arun then goes to work on his scooter, while Kamal
catches a bus for the city, where he attends an art
college. After they have gone, Bhabiji and Shobha
have their breakfast.

By nine o'clock everyone who is still in the house
is busy doing something. Shobha is washing clothes.
Bhabiji has settled down on a cot with a huge pile of

spinach, which she methodically cleans and chops up. Madhu, her fourteen-year-old granddaughter, who attends school only in the afternoons, is washing down the sitting room floor. Madhu's mother is a teacher in a primary school in Delhi, and earns a pittance of Rs 150 a month. Her husband went to England ten years ago, and never returned; he does not send any money home.

Madhu is made attractive by the gravity of her countenance. She is always thoughtful, reflective; seldom speaks, smiles rarely (but looks very pretty when she does). I wonder what she thinks about as she scrubs floors, prepares meals with Bhabiji, washes dishes and even finds a few hard-pressed moments for her school work. She is the Cinderella of the house. Not that she has to put up with anything like a cruel stepmother. Madhu is Bhabiji's favourite. She has made herself so useful that she is above all reproach. Apart from that, there is a certain measure of aloofness about her—she does not get involved in domestic squabbles—and this is foreign to a household in which everyone has something to say for himself or herself. Her two young brothers are constantly being reprimanded; but no one says anything to Madhu. Only yesterday morning, when clothes were being washed and Madhu was scrubbing the floor, the following dialogue took place.

Madhu's mother (picking up a school book left in the courtyard), 'Where's that boy Popat? See how careless he is with his books! Popat! He's run off. Just wait till he gets back. I'll give him a good beating.'

Vinod's mother, 'It's not Popat's book. It's Vinod's. Where's Vinod?'

Vinod (grumpily), 'It's Madhu's book.'

Silence for a minute or two. Madhu continues scrubbing the floor; she does not bother to look up. Vinod picks up the book and takes it indoors. The women return to their chores.

Manju, daughter of Shiv and sister of Vinod, is averse to housework and, as a result, is always being scolded—by her parents, grandmother, uncles and aunts.

Now, she is engaged in the unwelcome chore of sweeping the front yard. She does this with a sulky look, ignoring my cheerful remarks. I have been sitting under the guava tree, but Manju soon sweeps me away from this spot. She creates a drifting cloud of dust, and seems satisfied only when the dust

settles on the clothes that have just been hung up to
dry. Manju is a sensuous creature and, like most
sensuous people, is lazy by nature. She does not like
sweeping because the boy next door can see her at it,
and she wants to appear before him in a more
glamorous light. Her first action every morning is to
turn to the cinema advertisements in the newspaper.
Bombay's movie moguls cater for girls like Manju
who long to be tragic heroines. Life is so very dull
for middle-class teenagers in Delhi that it is only
natural that they should lean so heavily on escapist
entertainment. Every residential area has a cinema.
But there is not a single bookshop in this particular
suburb, although it has a population of over twenty
thousand literate people. Few children read books;
but they are adept at swotting up examination
'guides'; and students of, say, Hardy or Dickens,
read the guides and not the novels.

Bhabiji is now grinding onions and chillies in a
mortar. Her eyes are watering but she is in a good
mood. Shobha sits quietly in the kitchen. A little
while ago she was complaining to me of a backache.
I am the only one who lends a sympathetic ear to
complaints of aches and pains. But since last night,
my sympathies have been under severe strain. When

I got into bed at about ten o'clock, I found the sheets wet. Apparently, Shobha had put her baby to sleep in my bed during the afternoon.

While the housework is still in progress, cousin Kishore arrives. He is an itinerant musician who makes a living by arranging performances at marriages. He visits Bhabiji's house frequently and at odd hours, often a little tipsy, always brimming over with goodwill and grandiose plans for the future. It was once his ambition to be a film producer, and some years back he lost a lot of Bhabiji's money in producing a film that was never completed. He still talks of finishing it.

'Brother,' he says, taking me into his confidence for the hundredth time, 'do you know anyone who has a movie camera?'

'No,' I say, knowing only too well how these admissions can lead me into a morass of complicated manoeuvres. But Kishore is not easily put off, specially when he has been fortified with country liquor.

'But you *knew* someone with a movie camera?' he asks.

'That was long ago.'

'How long ago?' (I have got him going now.)

'About five years back.'

'Only five years? Find him, find him!'

'It's no use. He doesn't have the movie camera any more. He sold it.'

'Sold it!' Kishore looks at me as though I have done him an injury. 'But why didn't you buy it? All we need is a movie camera, and our fortune is made. I will produce the film, I will direct it, I will write the music. Two in one, Charlie Chaplin and Raj Kapoor. Why didn't you buy the camera?'

'Because I didn't have the money.'

'But we could have borrowed the money.'

'If you are in a position to borrow money, you can go out and buy another movie camera.'

'We could have borrowed the camera. Do you know anyone else who has one?'

'Not a soul.' I am firm this time; I will not be led into another maze.

'Very sad, very sad,' mutters Kishore. And with a dejected, hangdog expression designed to make me feel that I am responsible for all his failures, he moves off.

Bhabiji had expressed some annoyance at his arrival, but he softens her up by leaving behind an invitation to a marriage party this evening. No one in the house knows the bride's or bridegroom's family, but that does not matter; knowing one of the musicians is just as good. Almost everyone will go.

While Bhabiji, Shobha and Madhu are preparing lunch, Bhabiji engages in one of her favourite subjects of conversation, Kamal's marriage, which she hopes she will be able to arrange in the near future. She freely acknowledges that she made grave blunders in selecting wives for her other sons—this is meant to be heard by Shobha—and promises not to repeat her mistakes. According to Bhabiji, Kamal's bride should be both educated and domesticated; and, of course, she must be fair.

'What if he likes a dark girl?' I ask teasingly.

Bhabiji looks horrified. 'He cannot marry a dark girl,' she declares.

'But dark girls are beautiful,' I tell her.

'Impossible!'

'Do you want him to marry a European girl?'

'No foreigners! I know them, they'll take my son away. He shall have a good Punjabi girl, with a complexion the colour of wheat.'

Noon. The shadows shift and cross the road. I sit beneath the guava tree and watch the women at work. They will not let me do anything, but they like talking to me and they love to hear my broken Punjabi. Sparrows flit about at their feet, snapping up the grain that runs away from their busy fingers. A crow looks speculatively at the empty kitchen, sidles towards the open door; but Bhabiji has only to glance up and the experienced crow flies away. He knows he will not be able to make off with anything from this house.

One by one the children come home, demanding food. Now it is Madhu's turn to go to school. Her younger brother, Popat, an intelligent but undersized boy of thirteen, appears in the doorway and asks for lunch.

'Be off!' says Bhabiji. 'It isn't ready yet.'

Actually the food is ready and only the chapattis remain to be made. Shobha will attend to them. Bhabiji lies down on her cot in the sun, complaining of a pain in her back and ringing noises in her ears.

'I'll press your back,' says Popat. He has been out of Bhabiji's favour lately, and is looking for an opportunity to be rehabilitated.

Barefooted he stands on Bhabiji's back and treads her weary flesh and bones with a gentle walking-in-one-spot movement. Bhabiji grunts with relief. Every day she has new pains in new places. Her age, and the daily business of feeding the family and running everyone's affairs, are beginning to tell on her. But she would sooner die than give up her position of dominance in the house. Her working sons still hand over their pay to her, and she dispenses the money as she sees fit.

The pummelling she gets from Popat puts her in a better mood, and she holds forth on another favourite subject, the respective merits of various dowries. Shiv's wife (according to Bhabiji) brought nothing with her but a string cot; Kishore's wife brought only a sharp and clever tongue; Shobha brought a wonderful steel cupboard, fully expecting that it would do all the housework for her.

This last observation upsets Shobha, and a little later I find her under the guava tree, weeping profusely. I give her the comforting words she obviously expects; but it is her husband, Arun, who will have to bear the brunt of her outraged feelings when he comes home this evening. He is rather nervous of his wife. Last night he wanted to eat out, at a restaurant, but did not want to be accused of wasting money; so he stuffed fifteen rupees into my pocket and asked me to invite both him and Shobha

to dinner, which I did. We had a good dinner. Such
unexpected hospitality on my part has further
improved my standing with Shobha. Now, in spite
of other chores, she sees that I get cups of tea and
coffee at odd hours of the day.

Bhabiji knows Arun is soft with his wife, and
taunts him about it. She was saying this morning
that whenever there is any work to be done, Shobha
retires to bed with a headache (party true). She says
even Manju does more housework (not true).
Bhabiji has certain talents as an actress, and does a
good take-off of Shobha sulking and grumbling at
having too much to do.

While Bhabiji talks, Popat sneaks off and goes
for a ride on the bicycle. It is a very old bicycle and is
constantly undergoing repairs. 'The soul has gone
out of it,' says Vinod philosophically and makes his
way on to the roof, where he keeps a store of
pornographic literature. Up there, he cannot be seen
and cannot be remembered, and so avoids being
sent out on errands.

One of the boys is bathing at the handpump.
Manju, who should have gone to school with
Madhu, is stretched out on a cot, complaining of
fever. But she will be up in time to attend the

marriage party . . .

Towards evening, as the birds return to roost in the guava tree, their chatter is challenged by the tumult of people in the house getting ready for the marriage party.

Manju presses her tight pyjamas but neglects to darn them. She wears a loose-fitting, diaphanous shirt. She keeps flitting in and out of the front room so that I can admire the way she glitters. Shobha has used too much powder and lipstick in an effort to look like the femme fatale which she indubitably is not. Shiv's more conservative wife floats around in loose, old-fashioned pyjamas. Bhabiji is sober and austere in a white sari. Madhu looks neat. The men wear their suits.

Popat is holding up a mirror for his Uncle Kishore, who is combing his long hair. (Kishore kept his hair long; like a court musician at the time of Akbar, before the hippies had been heard of.) He is nodding benevolently, having fortified himself from a bottle labelled 'Som Ras' ('Nectar of the Gods'), obtained cheaply from an illicit still.

Kishore: 'Don't shake the mirror, boy!'

Popat: 'Uncle, it's your head that's shaking.'

Shobha is happy. She loves going out, specially

to marriages, and she always takes her two small boys with her, although they invariably spoil the carpets.

Only Kamal, Popat and I remain behind. I have had more than my share of marriage parties.

The house is strangely quiet. It does not seem so small now, with only three people left in it. The kitchen has been locked (Bhabiji will not leave it open while Popat is still in the house), so we visit the dhaba, the wayside restaurant near the main road, and this time I pay the bill with my own money. We have kababs and chicken curry.

Yesterday, Kamal and I took our lunch on the grass of the Buddha Jayanti Gardens (Buddha's Birthday Gardens). There was no college for Kamal, as the majority of Delhi's students had hijacked a number of corporation buses and headed for the Pakistan High Commission, with every intention of levelling it to the ground if possible, as a protest against the hijacking of an Indian plane from Srinagar to Lahore. The students were met by the Delhi police in full strength, and a pitched battle took place, in which stones from the students and tear-gas shells from the police were the favoured missiles. There were two shells fired every minute, according to a newspaper report. And this went on all day. A number of students and policemen were injured, but by some miracle no one was killed. The police held their ground, and the Pakistan High Commission remained inviolate. But the Australian High Commission, situated to the rear of the student brigade, received most of the tear-gas shells, and had to close down for the day.

Kamal and I attended the siege for about an hour, before retiring to the Gardens with our ham sandwiches. A couple of friendly squirrels came up to investigate, and were soon taking bread from our hands. We could hear the chanting of the students in the distance. I lay back on the grass and opened my copy of *Barchester Towers*. Whenever life in Delhi, or in Bhabiji's house (or anywhere, for that matter), becomes too tumultuous, I turn to Trollope. Nothing could be further removed from the turmoil of our times than an English cathedral town in the nineteenth century. But I think Jane Austen would have appreciated life in Bhabiji's house.

By ten o'clock, everyone is back from the marriage. (They had gone for the feast, and not for the ceremonies, which continue into the early hours of the morning.) Shobha is full of praise for the bridegroom's good looks and fair complexion. She describes him as being 'gora-chitta'—very white! She does not have a high opinion of the bride.

Shiv, in a happy and reflective mood, extols the qualities of his own wife, referring to her as The Barrel. He tells us how, shortly after their marriage, she had threatened to throw a brick at the next-door girl. This little incident remains fresh in Shiv's mind, after eighteen years of marriage.

He says, 'When the neighbours came and complained, I told them, "It is quite possible that my wife will throw a brick at your daughter. She is in the habit of throwing bricks." The neighbours held their peace.'

I think Shiv is rather proud of his wife's militancy when it comes to taking on neighbours; recently, she vanquished the woman next door (a formidable Sikh lady) after a verbal battle that lasted three hours. But in arguments or quarrels with Bhabiji, Shiv's wife always loses, because Shiv takes his mother's side.

Arun, on the other hand, is afraid of both his wife and mother, and simply makes himself scarce when a quarrel develops. Or he tells his mother she is right, and then, to placate Shobha, takes her to the pictures.

Kishore turns up just as everyone is about to go to bed. Bhabiji is annoyed at first, because he has been drinking too much; but when he produces a bunch of cinema tickets, she is mollified and asks him to stay the night. Not even Bhabiji likes missing a new picture.

Kishore is urging me to write his life story.

'Your life would make a most interesting story,' I tell him. 'But it will be interesting only if I put in everything—your successes *and* your failures.'

'No, no, only successes,' exhorts Kishore. 'I want you to describe me as a popular music director.'

'But you have yet to become popular.'

'I will be popular if you write about me.'

Fortunately, we are interrupted by the cots being brought in. Then Bhabiji and Shiv go into a huddle, discussing plans for building an extra room. After all, Kamal may be married soon.

One by one, the children get under their quilts. Popat starts massaging Bhabiji's back. She gives him her favourite blessing, 'God protect you and give you lots of children.' If God listens to all Bhabiji's prayers and blessings, there will never be a fall in the population.

The lights are off and Bhabiji settles down for the night. She is almost asleep when a small voice pipes up, 'Bhabiji, tell us a story.'

At first Bhabiji pretends not to hear; then, when the request is repeated, she says, 'You'll keep Aunty Shobha awake, and then she'll have an excuse for getting up late in the morning.' But the children know Bhabiji's one great weakness, and they renew their demand.

'Your grandmother is tired,' says Arun. 'Let her sleep.'

But Bhabiji's eyes are open. Her mind is going back over the crowded years, and she remembers something very interesting that happened when her younger brother's wife's sister married the eldest son of her third cousin . . .

Before long, the children are asleep, and I am wondering if I will ever sleep, for Bhabiji's voice drones on, into the darker reaches of the night.

# Uncle Bill—He Said it With Arsenic

Is there such a person as a born murderer—in the sense that there are born writers and musicians, born winners and losers?

One can't be sure. The urge to do away with troublesome people is common to most of us, but only a few succumb to it. If ever there was a born murderer, he must surely have been William Jones. The thing came so naturally to him. No extreme violence, no messy shootings or hackings or throttling; just the right amount of poison, administered with skill and discretion.

A gentle, civilized sort of person was Mr Jones. He collected butterflies and arranged them systematically in glass cases. His ether bottle was quick and painless. He never stuck pins into the beautiful creatures.

Have you ever heard of the Agra Double Murder? It happened, of course, a great many years ago, when Agra was a far-flung outpost of the British Empire. In those days, William Jones was a male nurse in one of the city's hospitals. The patients—specially terminal cases—spoke highly of the care and consideration he showed them. While most nurses, both male and female, preferred to attend to the more hopeful cases, nurse William was always prepared to stand duty over a dying patient.

He felt a certain empathy for the dying; he liked to see them on their way. It was just his good nature, of course.

On a visit to nearby Meerut, he met and fell in love with Mrs Browning, the wife of the local Stationmaster. Impassioned love letters were soon putting a strain on the Agra-Meerut postal service. The envelopes grew heavier—not so much because the letters were growing longer but because they contained little packets of a powdery white substance, accompanied by detailed instructions as to its correct administration.

Mr Browning, an unassuming and trustful man—one of the world's born losers, in fact—was not the sort to read his wife's correspondence. Even when he was seized by frequent attacks of colic, he put them down to an impure water supply. He recovered from one bout of vomiting and diarrhoea only to be racked by another.

He was hospitalized on a diagnosis of gastroenteritis; and, thus freed from his wife's ministrations, soon got better. But on returning home and drinking a glass of nimbu pani brought to him by the solicitous Mrs Browning, he had a relapse from which he did not recover.

Those were the days when deaths from cholera and related diseases were only too common in India, and death certificates were easier to obtain than dog licences.

After a short interval of mourning (it was the hot weather and you couldn't wear black for long), Mrs Browning moved to Agra, where she rented a house next door to William Jones.

I forgot to mention that Mr Jones was also married. His wife was an insignificant creature, no match for a genius like William. Before the hot weather was over, the dreaded cholera had taken her too. The way was clear for the lovers to unite in holy matrimony.

But Dame Gossip lived in Agra too, and it was not long before tongues were wagging and anonymous letters were being received by the superintendent of police. Inquiries were instituted. Like most infatuated lovers, Mrs Browning had hung on to her beloved's letters and billet-doux, and these soon came to light. The silly woman had kept them in a box beneath her bed.

Exhumations were ordered in both Agra and Meerut.

Arsenic keeps well, even in the hottest of weather, and there was no dearth of it in the remains of both victims.

Mr Jones and Mrs Browning were arrested and charged with murder.

'Is Uncle Bill really a murderer?' I asked from the drawing room sofa in my grandmother's house in Dehra. (It's time that I told you that William Jones was my uncle, my mother's half brother.)

I was eight or nine at the time. Uncle Bill had spent the previous summer with us in Dehra and had stuffed me with bazaar sweets and pastries, all of which I had consumed without suffering any ill effects.

'Who told you that about Uncle Bill?' asked Grandmother.

'I heard it in school. All the boys were asking me the same question—"Is your uncle a murderer?" They say he poisoned both his wives.'

'He had only one wife,' snapped Aunt Mabel.

'Did he poison her?'

'No, of course not. How can you say such a thing!'

'Then why is Uncle Bill in gaol?'

'Who says he's in gaol?'

'The boys at school. They heard it from their parents. Uncle Bill is to go on trial in the Agra fort.'

There was a pregnant silence in the drawing room, then Aunt Mabel burst out, 'It was all that awful woman's fault.'

'Do you mean Mrs Browning?' asked Grandmother.

'Yes, of course. She must have put him up to it. Bill couldn't have thought of anything so—so diabolical!'

'But he sent her the powders, dear. And don't forget—Mrs Browning has since . . .'

Grandmother stopped in mid-sentence, and both she and Aunt Mabel glanced surreptitiously at me.

'Committed suicide,' I filled in. 'There were still some powders with her.'

Aunt Mabel's eyes rolled heavenwards. 'This boy is impossible. I don't know what he will be like when he grows up.'

'At least I won't be like Uncle Bill,' I said. 'Fancy poisoning people! If I kill anyone, it will be in a fair fight. I suppose they'll hang Uncle?'

'Oh, I hope not!'

Grandmother was silent. Uncle Bill was her stepson but she did have a soft spot for him. Aunt Mabel, his sister, thought he was wonderful. I had always considered him to be a bit soft but had to admit that he was generous. I tried to imagine him dangling at the end of a hangman's rope, but somehow he didn't fit the picture.

As things turned out, he didn't hang. During the Raj, White people in India seldom got the death sentence, although the hangman was pretty busy disposing of dacoits and political terrorists. Uncle Bill was given a life sentence and settled down to a sedentary job in the prison library at Naini, near Allahabad. His gifts as a male nurse went unappreciated; they did not trust him in the hospital.

He was released after seven or eight years, shortly after the country became an independent Republic. He came out of gaol to find that the British were leaving, either for England or the remaining colonies. Grandmother was dead. Aunt Mabel and her husband had settled in South Africa. Uncle Bill realized that there was little future for him in India and followed his sister out to Johannesburg.

I was in my last year at boarding school. After my father's death, my mother had married an Indian, and now my future lay in India.

I did not see Uncle Bill after his release from prison, and no one dreamt that he would ever turn up again in India.

In fact, fifteen years were to pass before he came back, and by then I was in my early thirties, the author of a book that had become something of a best-seller. The previous fifteen years had been a struggle—the sort of struggle that every young freelance writer experiences—but at last the hard work was paying off and the royalties were beginning to come in.

I was living in a small cottage on the outskirts of the hill station of Fosterganj; working on another book, when I received an unexpected visitor.

He was a thin, stooped, grey-haired man in his late fifties, with a straggling moustache and discoloured teeth. He looked feeble and harmless but for his eyes which were pale cold blue. There was something slightly familiar about him.

'Don't you remember me?' he asked. 'Not that I really expect you to, after all these years . . .'

'Wait a minute. Did you teach me at school?'

'No—but you're getting warm.' He put his suitcase down and I glimpsed his name on the airlines label. I looked up in astonishment. 'You're not—you couldn't be . . .'

'Your Uncle Bill,' he said with a grin and extended his hand. 'None other!' And he sauntered into the house.

I must admit that I had mixed feelings about his arrival. While I had never felt any dislike for him, I hadn't exactly approved of what he had done. Poisoning, I felt, was a particularly reprehensible way of getting rid of inconvenient people: not that I could think of any commendable ways of getting rid of them! Still, it had happened a long time ago, he'd been punished, and presumably he was a reformed character.

'And what have you been doing all these years?' he asked me, easing himself into the only comfortable chair in the room.

'Oh just writing,' I said.

'Yes, I heard about your last book. It's quite a success, isn't it?'

'It's doing quite well. Have you read it?'

'I don't do much reading.'

'And what have you been doing all these years,

Uncle Bill?'

'Oh, knocking about here and there. Worked for a soft-drink company for some time. And then with a drug firm. My knowledge of chemicals was useful.'

'Weren't you with Aunt Mabel in South Africa?'

'I saw quite a lot of her, until she died a couple of years ago. Didn't you know?'

'No. I've been out of touch with relatives.' I hoped he'd take that as a hint. 'And what about her husband?'

'Died too, not long after. Not many of us left, my boy. That's why, when I saw something about you in the papers, I thought why not go and see my only nephew again?'

'You're welcome to stay a few days,' I said quickly. 'Then I have to go to Bombay.' (This was a lie, but I did not relish the prospect of looking after Uncle Bill for the rest of his days.)

'Oh, I won't be staying long,' he said. 'I've got a bit of money put by in Johannesburg. It's just that so far as I know you're my only living relative, and I thought it would be nice to see you again.'

Feeling relieved, I set about trying to make Uncle Bill as comfortable as possible. I gave him my bedroom and turned the window seat into a bed for myself. I was a hopeless cook but, using all my ingenuity, I scrambled some eggs for supper. He waved aside my apologies; he'd always been a frugal eater, he said. Eight years in gaol had given him a cast-iron stomach.

He did not get in my way but left me to my writing and my lonely walks. He seemed content to sit in the spring sunshine and smoke his pipe.

It was during our third evening together that he said, 'Oh, I almost forgot. There's a bottle of sherry in my suitcase. I brought it specially for you.'

'That was very thoughtful of you, Uncle Bill. How did you know I was fond of sherry?'

'Just my intuition. You do like it, don't you?'

'There's nothing like a good sherry.'

He went to his bedroom and came back with an unopened bottle of South African sherry.

'Now you just relax near the fire,' he said agreeably. 'I'll open the bottle and fetch glasses.'

He went to the kitchen while I remained near the electric fire, flipping through some journals. It seemed to me that Uncle Bill was taking rather a long time. Intuition must be a family trait, because it came to me quite suddenly—the thought that Uncle

Bill might be intending to poison me.

After all, I thought, here he is after nearly fifteen years, apparently for purely sentimental reasons. But I had just published a best-seller. And I was his nearest relative. If I were to die, Uncle Bill could lay claim to my estate and probably live comfortably on my royalties for the next five or six years!

What had really happened to Aunt Mabel and her husband, I wondered. And where did Uncle Bill get the money for an air ticket to India?

Before I could ask myself any more questions, he reappeared with the glasses on a tray. He set the tray on a small table that stood between us. The glasses had been filled. The sherry sparkled.

I stared at the glass nearest me, trying to make out if the liquid in it was cloudier than that in the other glass. But there appeared to be no difference.

I decided I would not take any chances. It was a round tray, made of smooth Kashmiri walnut wood. I turned it round with my index finger, so that the glasses changed places.

'Why did you do that?' asked Uncle Bill.

'It's a custom in these parts. You turn the tray with the sun, a complete revolution. It brings good luck.'

Uncle Bill looked thoughtful for a few moments, then said, 'Well, let's have some more luck,' and turned the tray around again.

'Now you've spoilt it,' I said. 'You're not supposed to keep revolving it! That's bad luck. I'll have to turn it about again to cancel out the bad luck.'

The tray swung round once more, and Uncle Bill had the glass that was meant for me.

'Cheers!' I said, and drank from my glass.

It was good sherry. Uncle Bill hesitated. Then he shrugged, said 'Cheers', and drained his glass quickly.

But he did not offer to fill the glasses again.

Early next morning he was taken violently ill. I heard him retching in his room, and I got up and went to see if there was anything I could do. He was groaning, his head hanging over the side of the bed. I brought him a basin and a jug of water.

'Would you like me to fetch a doctor?' I asked.

He shook his head. 'No, I'll be all right. It must be something I ate.'

'It's probably the water. It's not too good at this time of the year. Many people come down with gastric trouble during their first few days in

Fosterganj.'

'Ah, that must be it,' he said, and doubled up as a fresh spasm of pain and nausea swept over him.

He was better by the evening—whatever had gone into the glass must have been by way of the preliminary dose, and a day later he was well enough to pack his suitcase and announce his departure. The climate of Fosterganj did not agree with him, he told me.

Just before he left, I said, 'Tell me, Uncle, why did you drink it?'

'Drink what? The water?'

'No, the glass of sherry into which you'd slipped one of your famous powders.'

He gaped at me, then gave a nervous whinnying laugh. 'You will have your little joke, won't you?'

'No, I mean it,' I said. 'Why did you drink the stuff? It was meant for me, of course.'

He looked down at his shoes, then gave a little shrug and turned away.

'In the circumstances,' he said, 'it seemed the only decent thing to do.'

I'll say this for Uncle Bill: he was always the perfect gentleman.

## Prem

'And the last puff of the day-wind brought
from the unseen villages, the scent of damp
wood-smoke, hot cakes, dripping
undergrowth, and rotting pine-cones. That
is the true smell of the Himalayas, and if once
it creeps into the blood of a man, that man
will at the last, forgetting all else, return to
the hills to die.'

— Rudyard Kipling

On the first clear September day, towards the end of
the rains, I visited the pine knoll, my place of peace
and power . . .

This is where I will write my stories. I can see
everything from here—my cottage across the valley;
behind and above me, the town and the bazaar,
straddling the ridge; to the left, the high mountains
and the twisting road to the source of the great river;
below me, the little stream and the path to the
village; ahead, the Hill of Fairies, the fields beyond;
the wide valley below, and then another range of

---

Extract from *From Small Beginnings*

hills and then the distant plains. I can even see Prem Singh in the garden, putting the mattresses out in the sun.

From here he is just a speck on the far hill, but I know it is Prem by the way he stands. A man may have a hundred disguises, but in the end it is his posture that gives him away. Like my grandfather, who was a master of disguise and successfully roamed the bazaars as fruit vendor or basket-maker; but we could always recognize him because of his pronounced slouch.

Prem Singh doesn't slouch, but he has this habit of looking up at the sky (regardless of whether it's cloudy or clear), and at the moment he's looking at the sky.

Eight years with Prem. He was just a sixteen-year-old boy when I first saw him, and now he has a wife and child.

I had been in the cottage for just over a year . . . He stood on the landing outside the kitchen door. A tall boy, dark, with good teeth and brown, deep-set eyes; dressed smartly in white drill—his only change of clothes. Looking for a job. I liked the look of him. But—

'I already have someone working for me,' I said.

'Yes, sir. He is my uncle.'

In the hills, everyone is a brother or uncle.

'You don't want me to dismiss your uncle?'

'No, sir. But he says you can find a job for me.'

'I'll try. I'll make inquiries. Have you just come from your village?'

'Yes. Yesterday I walked ten miles to Pauri. There I got a bus.'

'Sit down. Your uncle will make some tea.'

He sat down on the steps, removed his white keds, wriggled his toes. His feet were both long and broad; large feet, but not ugly. He was unusually clean for a hill boy. And taller than most.

'Do you smoke?' I asked.

'No, sir.'

'It is true,' said his uncle, 'he does not smoke. All my nephews smoke, but this one, he is a little peculiar, he does not smoke—neither beedi nor hookah.'

'Do you drink?'

'It makes me vomit.'

'Do you take bhang?'

'No, sahib.'

'You have no vices. It's unnatural.'

'He is unnatural, sahib,' said his uncle.

'Does he chase girls?'

'They chase him, sahib.'

'So he left the village and came looking for a job.' I looked at him. He grinned, then looked away, began rubbing his feet.

'Your name is?'

'Prem Singh.'

'All right, Prem, I will try to do something for you.'

I did not see him for a couple of weeks. I forgot about finding him a job. But when I met him again, on the road to the bazaar, he told me that he had got a temporary job in the Survey, looking after the surveyor's tents.

'Next week we will be going to Rajasthan,' he said.

'It will be very hot. Have you been in the desert before?'

'No, sir.'

'It is not like the hills. And it is far from home.'

'I know. But I have no choice in the matter. I have to collect some money in order to get married.'

In his region there was a bride price, usually of two thousand rupees.

'Do you have to get married so soon?'

'I have only one brother and he is still very young. My mother is not well. She needs a daughter-in-law to help her in the fields and with the cows and in the house. We are a small family, so the work is greater.'

Every family has its few terraced fields, narrow and stony, usually perched on a hillside above a stream or river . . . There is no money to be earned in the villages, and money is needed for clothes, soap, medicines, and recovering the family jewellery from the moneylenders. So the young men leave their villages to find work, and to find work they must go to the plains. The lucky ones get into the army. Others enter domestic service or take jobs in garages, hotels, wayside teashops, schools . . .

In Mussoorie, the main attraction is the large number of schools, which employ cooks and bearers. But the schools were full when Prem arrived. He'd been to the recruiting centre at Roorkee, hoping to get into the army; but they found a deformity in his right foot, the result of a bone broken when a landslip carried him away one dark monsoon night. He was very lucky, he said, that it was only his foot and not his head that had been broken.

He came to the house to inform his uncle about the job and to say goodbye. I thought: another nice person I probably won't see again; another ship passing in the night, the friendly twinkle of its lights soon vanishing in the darkness. I said 'Come again,' held his smile with mine so that I could remember him better, and returned to my study and my typewriter.

Prem goes, disappears into the vast faceless cities of the plains, and a year slips by, or rather I do, and then here he is again, thinner and darker and still smiling and still looking for a job. I should have known that hill men don't disappear for ever. The spirit-haunted rocks don't let their people wander too far, lest they lose them forever.

I was able to get him a job in the school. The Headmaster's wife needed a cook. I wasn't sure if Prem could cook very well but I sent him along and they said they'd give him a trial. Three days later the Headmaster's wife met me on the road and started gushing all over me. She was the type who gushes.

'We're so grateful to you! Thank you for sending me that lovely boy. He's so polite. And he cooks very well. A little too hot for my husband, but otherwise delicious—just delicious! He's a real treasure—a lovely boy.' And she gave me an arch look—the famous look which she used to captivate all the good-looking young prefects who became prefects, it was said, only if she approved of them.

I wasn't sure if she didn't want something more than a cook, and I only hoped that Prem would give every satisfaction.

He looked cheerful enough when he came to see me on his off day.

'How are you getting on?' I asked.

'Lovely,' he said, using his mistress's favourite expression. 'What do you mean—lovely? Do they like your work?'

'The memsahib likes it. She strokes me on the cheek whenever she enters the kitchen. The sahib says nothing. He takes medicine after every meal.'

'Did he always take medicine—or only now that you're doing the cooking?'

'I am not sure. I think he has always been sick.'

He was sleeping in the Headmaster's veranda and getting sixty rupees a month. A cook in Delhi got a hundred and sixty. And a cook in Paris or New York got ten times as much. I did not say as much to Prem. He might ask me to get him a job in New

York. And that would be the last I saw of him!

'Prem,' I said. 'Why don't you work for me?'

'And what about my uncle?'

'He seems ready to desert me any day. His grandfather is ill, he says, and he wants to go home.'

'His grandfather died last year.'

'That's what I mean—he's getting restless. And I don't mind if he goes. These days he seems to be suffering from a form of sleeping sickness. I have to get up first and make his tea . . .'

Sitting here under the cherry tree, whose leaves are just beginning to turn yellow, I rest my chin on my knees and gaze across the valley to where Prem moves about in the garden. Looking back over the seven years he has been with me, I recall some of the nicest things about him. They come to me in no particular order—just pieces of cinema—coloured slides slipping across the screen of memory . . .

Prem rocking his infant son to sleep—crooning to him, passing his large hand gently over the child's curly head—Prem following me down to the police station when I was arrested*, and waiting outside

---

* On a warrant from Bombay, charging me with writing an allegedly obscene short story!

until I reappeared—his smile, when I found him in Delhi—his large, irrepressible laughter, most in evidence when he was seeing an old Laurel and Hardy movie.

Of course there were times when he could be infuriating, stubborn, deliberately pig-headed, sending me little notes of resignation—but I never found it difficult to overlook these little acts of self-indulgence. He had brought much love and laughter into my life, and what more could a lonely man ask for?

It was his stubborn streak that limited the length of his stay in the Headmaster's household. Mr Good was tolerant enough. But Mrs Good was one of those women who, when they are pleased with you, go out of their way to help, pamper and flatter; and who, when they are displeased, become vindictive, going out of their way to harm or destroy. Mrs Good sought power—over her husband, her dog, her favourite pupils, her servant . . . She had absolute power over the husband and the dog; partial power over her slightly bewildered pupils; and none at all over Prem, who missed the subtleties of her designs upon his soul. He did not respond to her mothering; or to the way in which she tweaked him on the cheeks, brushed against him in the kitchen, or made admiring remarks about his looks and physique.

Memsahibs, Prem knew, were not for him. So he kept a stony face and went diligently about his duties. And she felt slighted, put in her place. Her liking turned to dislike. Instead of admiring remarks, she began making disparaging remarks about his looks, his clothes, his manners. She found fault with his cooking. No longer was it 'lovely'. She even accused him of taking away the dog's meat and giving it to a poor family living on the hillside: no more heinous crime could be imagined! Mr Good threatened him with dismissal. So Prem became stubborn. The following day he withheld the dog's food altogether; threw it down the khud where it was seized upon by innumerable strays; and went off to the pictures.

It was the end of his job. 'I'll have to go home now,' he told me. 'I won't get another job in this area. The Mem will see to that.'

'Stay a few days,' I said.

'I have only enough money with which to get home.'

'Keep it for going home. You can stay with me

for a few days, while you look around. Your uncle won't mind sharing his food with you.'

His uncle did mind. He did not like the idea of working for his nephew as well; it seemed to him no part of his duties. And he was apprehensive lest Prem get his job.

So Prem stayed no longer than a week.

Here on the knoll the grass is just beginning to turn October yellow. The first clouds approaching winter cover the sky. The trees are very still. The birds are silent. Only a cricket keeps singing on the oak tree. Perhaps there will be a storm before evening. A storm like that in which Prem arrived at the cottage with his wife and child—but that's jumping too far ahead . . .

After he had returned to his village, it was several months before I saw him again. His uncle told me he had taken a job in Delhi. There was an address. It did not seem complete, but I resolved that when I was next in Delhi, I would try to see him.

The opportunity came in May, as the hot winds of summer blew across the plains.

Nothing went right for me. Of course the address was all wrong, and I wandered about in a remote, dusty, treeless colony called Vasant Vihar (Spring Garden) for over two hours, asking all the domestic servants I came across if they could put me in touch with Prem Singh of village Koli, Pauri Garhwal. There were innumerable Prem Singhs, but apparently none who belonged to village Koli. I returned to my hotel and took two days to recover from heatstroke before returning to Mussoorie, thanking God for mountains!

And then the uncle gave me notice. He'd found a better-paid job in Dehra Dun and was anxious to be off. I didn't try to stop him.

For the next six months I lived in the cottage without any help. I did not find this difficult. I was used to living alone. It wasn't service that I needed but companionship.

During the rains, watching the dripping trees and the mist climbing the valley, I wrote a great deal of poetry. But poetry didn't bring me much money, and funds were low. And then, just as I was wondering if I would have to give up my freedom and take a job again, a publisher bought the paperback rights of one of my children's stories, and I was free to live and write as I pleased—for another three months!

That was in November. To celebrate, I took a long walk through the Landour Bazaar and up the Tehri road. It was a good day for walking; and it was dark by the time I returned to the outskirts of the town. Someone stood waiting for me on the road above the cottage. I hurried past him.

> If I am not for myself,
> Who will be for me?
> And if I am not for others,
> What am I?
> And if not now, when?

I startled myself with the memory of these words of Hillel, the ancient Hebrew sage. I walked back to the shadows where the youth stood, and saw that it was Prem.

'Prem!' I said. 'Why are you sitting out here, in the cold? Why did you not go to the house?'

'I went, sir, but there was a lock on the door. I thought you had gone away.'

'And you were going to remain here, on the road?'

'Only for tonight. I would have gone down to

Dehra in the morning.'

'Come, let's go home. I have been waiting for you. I looked for you in Delhi, but could not find the place where you were working.'

'I have left them now.'

'And your uncle has left me. So will you work for me now?' 'For as long as you wish.'

'For as long as the gods wish.'

We did not go straight home, but returned to the bazaar and took our meal in the Sindhi Sweet Shop; hot puris and strong sweet tea.

We walked home together in the bright moonlight.

That was twenty years ago, and Prem, his wife and three children, and now three grandchildren, are still with me. But we live in a different house now, on another hill.

# Binya

Glow-worms shone fitfully in the dark. The night was full of sounds—the tonk-tonk of a nightjar, the cry of a barking-deer, the shuffling of porcupines, the soft flip-flop of moths beating against the windowpanes. On the hill across the valley, lights flickered in the small village—the dim lights of kerosene lamps swinging in the dark.

'What is your name?' I asked, when we met again on the path through the pine forest.

'Binya,' she said. 'What is yours?'

'I've no name.'

'All right, Mr No-name.'

'I mean I haven't made a name for myself. We must make our own names, don't you think?'

'Binya is my name. I do not wish to have any other. Where are you going?'

'Nowhere.'

'No-name goes nowhere! Then you cannot come with me, because I am going home and my grandmother will set the village dogs on you if you follow me.' And laughing, she ran down the path to

Extract from *Binya Passes By*

the stream; she knew I could not catch up with her.

Her face streamed summer rain as she climbed the steep hill, calling the white cow home. She seemed very tiny on the windswept mountainside; a twist of hair lay flat against her forehead, and her torn blue dhoti clung to her firm round thighs. I went to her with an umbrella to give her shelter. She stood with me beneath the umbrella and let me put my arm around her. Then she turned her face up to mine, wonderingly, and I kissed her quickly, softly on the lips. Her lips tasted of raindrops and mint. And then she left me there, so gallant in the blistering rain. She ran home laughing. But it was worth the drenching.

Another day I heard her calling to me— 'No-name, Mister No-name!'—but I couldn't see her, and it was some time before I found her, halfway up a cherry tree, her feet pressed firmly against the bark, her dhoti tucked up between her thighs—fair, rounded thighs, and legs that were strong and vigorous.

'The cherries are not ripe,' I said.

'They are never ripe. But I like them green and sour. Will you come into the tree?'

'If I can still climb a tree,' I said.

'My grandmother is over sixty, and *she* can climb trees.'

'Well, I wouldn't mind being more adventurous at sixty. There's not so much to lose then.' I climbed into the tree without much difficulty, but I did not think the higher branches would take my weight, so I remained standing in the fork of the tree, my face on a level with Binya's breasts. I put my hand against her waist, and kissed her on the soft inside of her arm. She did not say anything. But she took me by the hand and helped me to climb a little higher, and I put my arm around her, as much to support myself as to be close to her.

The full moon rides high, shining through the tall oak trees near the window. The night is full of sounds, crickets, the tonk-tonk of a nightjar, and floating across the valley from your village, the sound of drums beating, and people singing. It is a festival day, and there will be feasting in your home. Are you singing too, tonight? And are you thinking of me, as you sing, as you laugh, as you dance with your friends? I am sitting here alone, and so I have no one to think of but you.

Binya . . . I take your name again and again—as

though by taking it, I can make you hear me, come to me, walking over the moonlit mountain . . .

There are spirits abroad tonight. They move silently in the trees; they hover about the window at which I sit; they take up with the wind and rush about the house. Spirits of the trees, spirits of the old house. An old lady died here last year. She'd lived in the house for over thirty years; something of her personality surely dwells here still. When I look into the tall, old mirror which was hers, I sometimes catch a glimpse of her pale face and long, golden hair. She likes me, I think, and the house is kind to me. Would she be jealous of you, Binya?

The music and singing grows louder. I can imagine your face glowing in the firelight. Your eyes shine with laughter. You have all those people near you and I have only the stars, and the nightjar, and the ghost in the mirror.

I woke early, while the dew was still fresh on the grass, and walked down the hill to the stream, and then up to a little knoll where a pine tree grew in solitary splendour, the wind going *hoo-hoo* in its slender branches. This was my favourite place, my place of power, where I came to renew myself from time to time. I lay on the grass, dreaming. The sky in its blueness swung round above me. An eagle soared in the distance. I heard her voice down among the trees; or I thought I heard it. But when I went to look, I could not find her.

I'd always prided myself on my rationality; had taught myself to be wary of emotional states, like 'falling in love', which turned out to be ephemeral and illusory. And although I told myself again and again that the attraction was purely physical, on my part as well as hers, I had to admit to myself that my feelings towards Binya differed from the feelings I'd had for others; and that while sex had often been for me a celebration, it had, like any other feast, resulted in satiety, a need for change, a desire to forget . . .

Binya represented something else—something wild, dreamlike, fairy-like. She moved close to the spirit-haunted rocks, the old trees, the young grass; she had absorbed something from them—a primeval innocence, an unconcern with the passing of time and events, an affinity with the forest and the mountains; this made her special and magical.

And so, when three, four, five days went by, and I did not find her on the hillside, I went through all the pangs of frustrated love: had she forgotten me and gone elsewhere? Had we been seen together, and was she being kept at home? Was she ill? Or had she been spirited away?

I could hardly go and ask for her. I would probably be driven from the village. It straddled the opposite hill, a cluster of slate-roof houses, a pattern of little terraced fields. I could see figures in the fields, but they were too far away, too tiny, for me to be able to recognize anyone. She had gone to her mother's village a hundred miles away, or so, a small boy told me.

And so I brooded; walked disconsolately through the oak forest, hardly listening to the birds—the sweet-throated whistling thrush; the shrill barbet; the mellow-voiced doves. Happiness had always made me more responsive to nature. Feeling miserable, my thoughts turned inward. I brooded upon the trickery of time and circumstance; I felt the years were passing by, *had* passed by, like waves on a receding tide, leaving me washed up like a bit of flotsam on a lonely beach. But at the same time, the whistling thrush seemed to mock at me, calling tantalizingly from the shadows of the ravine, 'It isn't time that's passing by, it is you and I, it is you and I . . .'

Then I forced myself to snap out of my melancholy. I kept away from the hillside and the forest. I did not look towards the village. I buried myself in my work, tried to think objectively, and wrote an article on 'The inscriptions on the iron pillar at Kalsi'; very learned, very dry, very sensible.

But at night I was assailed by thoughts of Binya. I could not sleep. I switched on the light, and there she was, smiling at me from the looking glass, replacing the image of the old lady who had watched over me for so long.

# His Neighbour's Wife

'No (said Arun, as we waited for dinner to be prepared), I did not fall in love with my neighbour's wife. It is not that kind of story.

'Mind you, Leela was a most attractive woman. She was not beautiful or pretty but she was handsome. Hers was the firm, athletic body of a sixteen-year-old boy, free of any surplus flesh. She bathed morning and evening, oiling herself well, so that her skin glowed a golden-brown in the winter sunshine. Her lips were often coloured with paan juice, but her teeth were perfect.

'I was her junior by about five years, and she called me her "younger brother". Her husband, who was forty to her thirty-two, was an official in the Customs and Excise Department: an extrovert, a hard-drinking, backslapping man, who spent a great deal of time on tour. Leela knew that he was not always faithful to her during these frequent absences but she found solace in her own loyalty and in the well-being of her one child, a boy called Chandu.

'I did not care for the boy. He had been well spoilt, and took great delight in disturbing me whenever I was at work. He entered my rooms uninvited, knocked my books about, and, if guests were present, made insulting remarks about them to their faces.

'Leela, during her lonely evenings, would often ask me to sit on her veranda and talk to her. The day's work done, she would relax with a hookah. Smoking a hookah was a habit she had brought with her from her village near Agra, and it was a habit she refused to give up. She liked to talk and, as I was a good listener, she soon grew fond of me. The fact that I was twenty-six years old and still a bachelor, never failed to astonish her.

'It was not long before she took upon herself the responsibility for getting me married. I found it useless to protest. She did not believe me when I told her that I could not afford to marry, that I preferred a bachelor's life. A wife, she insisted, was an asset to any man. A wife reduced expenses. Where did I eat? At a hotel, of course. That must cost me at least sixty rupees a month, even on a vegetarian diet. But if I had a simple homely wife to do the cooking, we could both eat well for less than that.

'Leela fingered my shirt, observing that a button was missing and that the collar was frayed. She remarked on my pale face and general look of debility and told me that I would fall victim to all kinds of diseases if I did not find someone to look after me. What I needed, she declared between puffs at the hookah, was a woman—a young, healthy, buxom woman, preferably from a village near Agra.

'If I could find someone like you,' I said slyly, 'I would not mind getting married.'

'She appeared neither flattered nor offended by my remark.

'"Don't marry an older woman," she advised. "Never take a wife who is more experienced in the ways of the world than you are. You just leave it to me, I'll find a suitable bride for you."

'To please Leela, I agreed to this arrangement, thinking she would not take it seriously. But, two days later, when she suggested that I accompany her to a certain distinguished home for orphan girls, I became alarmed. I refused to have anything to do with her project.

'"Don't you have confidence in me?" she asked. "You said you would like a girl who resembled me. I know one who looks just as I did ten years ago."

'I like you as you are now,' I said. 'Not as you were ten years ago.'

'Of course. We shall arrange for you to see the girl first.'

'You don't understand,' I protested. 'It's not that I feel I have to be in love with someone before marrying her—I know you would choose a fine girl, and I would really prefer someone who is homely and simple to an MA with honours in psychology—it's just that I'm not ready for it. I want another year or two of freedom. I don't want to be chained down. To be frank, I don't want the responsibility.'

'"A little responsibility will make a man of you," said Leela; but she did not insist on my accompanying her to the orphanage, and the matter was allowed to rest for a few days.

'I was beginning to hope that Leela had reconciled herself to allowing one man to remain single in a world full of husbands when, one morning, she accosted me on the veranda with an open newspaper, which she thrust in front of my nose.

'"There!" she said triumphantly. "What do you think of that? I did it to surprise you."

'She had certainly succeeded in surprising me. Her henna-stained forefinger rested on an advertisement in the matrimonial columns.

'Bachelor journalist, age twenty-five, seeks attractive young wife well-versed in household duties Caste, religion no bar. Dowry optional.

'I must admit that Leela had made a good job of it. In a few days the replies began to come in, usually from the parents of the girls concerned. Each applicant wanted to know how much money I was earning. At the same time, they took the trouble to list their own connections and the high positions occupied by relatives. Some parents enclosed their daughters' photographs. They were very good photographs, though there was a certain amount of touching-up employed.

'I studied the pictures with interest. Perhaps marriage wasn't such a bad proposition, after all. I selected the photographs of the three girls I most fancied and showed them to Leela.

'To my surprise, she disapproved of all three. One of the girls, she said, had a face like a hermaphrodite; another obviously suffered from tuberculosis; and the third was undoubtedly an adventuress. Leela decided that the whole idea of the advertisement had been a mistake. She was sorry she had inserted it; the only replies we were likely to get would be from fortune hunters. And I had no fortune.

'So we destroyed the letters. I tried to keep some of the photographs, but Leela tore them up too.

'And so, for some time, there were no more attempts at getting me married.

'Leela and I met nearly every day, but we spoke of other things. Sometimes, in the evenings, she would make me sit on the charpoy opposite her, and then she would draw up her hookah and tell me stories about her village and her family. I was getting used to the boy, too, and even growing rather fond of him.

'All this came to an end when Leela's husband went and got himself killed. He was shot by a bootlegger who had decided to get rid of the excise man rather than pay him an exorbitant sum of money. It meant that Leela had to give up her quarters and return to her village near Agra. She waited until the boy's school-term had finished, and then she packed their things and bought two tickets, third-class to Agra.

'Something, I could see, had been troubling her, and when I saw her off at the station I realized what it was. She was having a fit of conscience about my continued bachelorhood.

'"In my village," she said confidently, leaning out from the carriage window, "there is a very comely young girl, a distant relative of mine. I shall speak to the parents."

'And then I said something which I had not considered before, which had never, until that moment, entered my head. And I was no less surprised than Leela when the words came tumbling out of my mouth, "Why don't *you* marry me now?"'

Arun didn't have time to finish his story because, just at this interesting stage, the dinner arrived.

But the dinner brought with it the end of his story.

It was served by his wife, a magnificent woman, strong and handsome, who could only have been Leela. And a few minutes later, Chandu, Arun's stepson, charged into the house, complaining that he was famished.

Arun introduced me to his wife, and we exchanged the usual formalities.

'But why hasn't your friend brought his family with him?' she asked.

'Family? Because he's still a bachelor!'

And then as he watched his wife's expression change from a look of mild indifference to one of deep concern, he hurriedly changed the subject.

# Kishen Again

Over the years, I was in and out of New Delhi's Regal Cinema quite a few times, and so I became used to meeting old acquaintances or glimpsing familiar faces in the foyer or on the steps outside.

On one occasion, I was mistaken for a ghost.

I was about thirty at the time. I was standing on the steps of the arcade, waiting for someone, when a young Indian man came up to me and said something in German or what sounded like German.

'I'm sorry,' I said. 'I don't understand. You may speak to me in English or Hindi.'

'Aren't you Hans? We met in Frankfurt last year.'

'I'm sorry, I've never been to Frankfurt.'

'You look exactly like Hans.'

'Maybe I'm his double. Or maybe I'm his ghost!'

My facetious remark did not amuse the young man. He looked confused and stepped back, a look of horror spreading over his face. 'No, no,' he stammered. 'Hans is alive, you can't be his ghost!'

---

Extract from *Reunion at the Regal*

'I was only joking.'

But he had turned away, hurrying off through the crowd. He seemed agitated. I shrugged philosophically. So I had a double called Hans, I reflected, perhaps I'd run into him some day.

I mention this incident only to show that most of us have lookalikes, and that sometimes we see what we *want* to see, or are looking for, even if on looking closer, the resemblance isn't all that striking.

But there was no mistaking Kishen when he approached me. I hadn't seen him for five or six years, but he looked much the same. Bushy eyebrows, offset by gentle eyes; a determined chin, offset by a charming smile. The girls had always liked him, and he knew it; and he was content to let them do the pursuing.

We saw a film—I think it was *The Wind Cannot Read*—and then we strolled across to the old Standard Restaurant, ordered dinner and talked about old times, while the small band played sentimental tunes from the 1950s.

Yes, we talked about old times—growing up in Dehra, where we lived next door to each other, exploring our neighbours' litchi orchards, cycling about the town in the days before the scooter had been invented, kicking a football around on the maidan, or just sitting on the compound wall doing nothing. I had just finished school, and an entire year stretched before me until it was time to go abroad. Kishen's father, a civil engineer, was under transfer orders, so Kishen too temporarily did not have to go to school.

He was an easygoing boy, quite content to be at a loose end in my company—I was to describe a couple of our escapades in my first novel, *The Room on the Roof*. I had literary pretensions; he was apparently without ambition although, as he grew older, he was to surprise me by his wide reading and erudition.

One day, while we were cycling along the bank of the Raipur canal, he skidded off the path and fell into the canal with his cycle. The water was only waist-deep; but it was quite swift, and I had to jump in to help him. There was no real danger, but we had some difficulty getting the cycle out of the canal.

Later, he learnt to swim.

But that was after I'd gone away . . .

Convinced that my prospects would be better in England, my mother packed me off to her relatives in Jersey, and it was to be four long years before I could return to the land I truly cared for. In that time, many of my Dehra friends had left the town; it wasn't a place where you could do much after finishing school. Kishen wrote to me from Calcutta, where he was at an engineering college. Then he was off to 'study abroad'. I heard from him from time to time. He seemed happy. He had an equable temperament and got on quite well with most people. He had a girlfriend too, he told me.

'But,' he wrote, 'you're my oldest and best friend. Wherever I go, I'll always come back to see you.'

And of course he did. We met several times while I was living in Delhi, and once we revisited Dehra together and walked down Rajpur Road and ate tikkees and golguppas behind the Clock Tower. But the old familiar faces were missing. The streets were overbuilt and overcrowded, and the litchi gardens were fast disappearing. After we got back to Delhi, Kishen accepted the offer of a job in Bombay. We kept in touch in desultory fashion, but our paths and our lives had taken different directions. He was busy nurturing his career with an engineering firm; I had retreated to the hills with radically different goals—to write and be free of the burden of a ten-to-five desk job.

Time went by, and I lost track of Kishen.

About a year ago, I was standing in the lobby of the India International Centre, when an attractive young woman in her mid-thirties came up to me and said, 'Hello, Rusty, don't you remember me? I'm Manju. I lived next to you and Kishen and Ranbir when we were children.'

I recognized her then, for she had always been a pretty girl, the 'belle' of Dehra's Astley Hall.

We sat down and talked about old times and new times, and I told her that I hadn't heard from Kishen for a few years.

'Didn't you know?' she asked. 'He died about two years ago.'

'What happened?' I was dismayed, even angry, that I hadn't heard about it. 'He couldn't have been more than thirty-eight.'

'It was an accident on a beach in Goa. A child had got into difficulties and Kishen swam out to save her. He did rescue the little girl, but when he swam ashore he had a heart attack. He died right there on the beach. It seems he had always had a weak heart. The exertion must have been too much for him.'

I was silent. I knew he'd become a fairly good swimmer, but I did not know about the heart.

'Was he married?' I asked.

'No, he was always the eligible bachelor boy.'

It had been good to see Manju again, even though she had given me bad news. She told me she was happily married, with a small son. We promised to keep in touch.

And that's the end of this tale, apart from my brief visit to Delhi last November.

I had taken a taxi to Connaught Place and decided to get down at the Regal. I stood there a while, undecided about what to do or where to go. It was almost time for a show to start, and there were a lot of people milling around.

I thought someone called my name. I looked around, and there was Kishen in the crowd. 'Kishen!' I called, and started after him.

But a stout lady climbing out of a scooter rickshaw got in my way, and by the time I had a clear view again, my old friend had disappeared.

Had I seen his lookalike, a double? Or had he kept his promise to come back to see me once more?

# Somi and Rusty

It was a sticky, restless afternoon. The water-carrier passed below the room with his skin bag, spraying water on the dusty path. The toy-seller entered the compound, calling his wares in a high-pitched sing-song voice, and presently there was the chatter of children.

The toy-seller had a long bamboo pole, crossed by two or three shorter bamboos, from which hung all manner of toys—little celluloid drums, tin watches, tiny flutes and whistles, and multicoloured rag dolls—and when these ran out, they were replaced by others from a large bag, a most mysterious and fascinating bag, one in which no one but the toy-seller was allowed to look. He was a popular person with the rich and poor alike, for his toys never cost more than four annas and never lasted longer than a day.

Rusty liked the cheap toys, and was fond of decorating the room with them. He bought a two-anna flute, and walked upstairs, blowing on it.

He removed his shirt and sandals and lay flat on

Extract from *The Room on the Roof*

the bed staring up at the ceiling. The lizards scuttled along the rafters, the bald maina hopped along the window ledge. He was about to fall asleep when Somi came into the room.

Somi looked listless.

'I feel sticky,' he said, 'I don't want to wear any clothes.'

He too pulled off his shirt and deposited it on the table, then stood before the mirror, studying his physique. Then he turned to Rusty.

'You don't look well,' he said, 'there are cobwebs in your hair.'

'I don't care.'

'You must have been very fond of Mrs Kapoor. She was very kind.'

'I loved her, didn't you know?'

'No. My own love is the only thing I know. Rusty, best favourite friend, you cannot stay here in this room, you must come back to my house. Besides, this building will soon have new tenants.'

'I'll get out when they come, or when the landlord discovers I'm living here.'

Somi's usually bright face was somewhat morose, and there was a faint agitation showing in his eyes.

'I will go and get a cucumber to eat,' he said, 'then there is something to tell you.'

'I don't want a cucumber,' said Rusty, 'I want a coconut.'

'I want a cucumber.'

Rusty felt irritable. The room was hot, the bed was hot, his blood was hot. Impatiently, he said, 'Go and eat your cucumber, I don't want any . . .'

Somi looked at him with a pained surprise; then, without a word, picked up his shirt and marched out of the room. Rusty could hear the slap of his slippers on the stairs, and then the bicycle tyres on the gravel path.

'Hey, Somi!' shouted Rusty, leaping off the bed and running out on to the roof. 'Come back!'

But the bicycle jumped over the ditch, and Somi's shirt flapped, and there was nothing Rusty could do but return to bed. He was alarmed at his liverish ill-temper. He lay down again and stared at the ceiling, at the lizards chasing each other across the rafters. On the roof two crows were fighting, knocking each other's feathers out. Everyone was in a temper.

What's wrong? wondered Rusty. I spoke to Somi in fever, not in anger, but my words were angry. Now I am miserable, fed up. Oh, hell . . .

He closed his eyes and shut out everything.

He opened his eyes to laughter. Somi's face was close, laughing into Rusty's.

'Of what were you dreaming, Rusty, I have never seen you smile so sweetly!'

'Oh, I wasn't dreaming,' said Rusty, sitting up, and feeling better now that Somi had returned. 'I am sorry for being so grumpy, but I'm not feeling . . .'

'Quiet!' admonished Somi, putting his finger to the other's lips. 'See I have settled the matter. Here is a coconut for you, and here is a cucumber for me!'

They sat cross-legged on the bed, facing each other; Somi with his cucumber, and Rusty with his coconut. The coconut milk trickled down Rusty's chin and on to his chest, giving him a cool, pleasant sensation.

Rusty said, 'I am afraid for Kishen. I am sure he will give trouble to his relatives, and they are not like his parents. Mr Kapoor will have no say, without Meena.'

Somi was silent. The only sound was the munching of the cucumber and the coconut. He looked at Rusty, an uncertain smile on his lips but none in his eyes; and, in a forced conversational manner, said, 'I'm going to Amritsar for a few months. But I will be back in the spring, Rusty, you will be all right here . . .'

This news was so unexpected that for some time Rusty could not take it in. The thought had never occurred to him that one day Somi might leave Dehra, just as Ranbir and Suri and Kishen had done. He could not speak. A sickening heaviness clogged his heart and brain.

'Hey, Rusty!' laughed Somi. 'Don't look as though there is poison in the coconut!'

The poison lay in Somi's words. And the poison worked, running through Rusty's veins and beating against his heart and hammering on his brain. The poison worked, wounding him.

He said, 'Somi . . .' but could go no further.

'Finish the coconut!'

'Somi,' said Rusty again, 'if you are leaving Dehra, Somi, then I am leaving too.'

'Eat the coco . . . what did you say?'

'I am going too.'

'Are you mad?'

'Not at all.'

Serious now, and troubled, Somi put his hand on his friend's wrist; he shook his head, he could not understand.

'Why, Rusty? Where?'

'England.'

'But you haven't money, you silly fool!'

'I can get an assisted passage. The British Government will pay.'

'You are a British subject?'

'I don't know . . .'

'*Toba!*' Somi slapped his thighs and looked upwards in despair. 'You are neither an Indian subject nor a British subject, and you think someone is going to pay for your passage! And how are you to get a passport?'

'How?' asked Rusty, anxious to find out.

'*Toba!* Have you a birth certificate?'

'Oh, no.'

'Then you are not born,' decreed Somi, with a certain amount of satisfaction. 'You are not alive! You do not happen to be in this world!'

He paused for breath, then waved his finger in the air. 'Rusty, you cannot go!' he said.

Rusty lay down despondently.

'I never really thought I would,' he said. 'I only said I would because I felt like it. Not because I am unhappy—I have never been happier elsewhere—

but because I am restless as I have always been. I don't suppose I'll be anywhere for long . . .'

He spoke the truth. Rusty always spoke the truth. He defined truth as feeling, and when he said what he felt, he said the truth. (Only he didn't always speak his feelings.) He never lied. You don't have to lie if you know how to withhold the truth.

'You belong here,' said Somi, trying to reconcile Rusty with the circumstance. 'You will get lost in big cities, Rusty, you will break your heart. And when you come back—if you come back—I will be grown-up and you will be grown-up—I mean more than we are now—and we will be like strangers to each other . . . And besides, there are no chaat shops in England!'

'But I don't belong here, Somi. I don't belong anywhere. Even if I have papers, I don't belong. I'm a half-caste, I know it, and that is as good as not belonging anywhere.'

What am I saying, thought Rusty, why do I make my inheritance a justification for my present bitterness? No one has cast me out . . . of my own free will I run away from India . . . why do I blame inheritance?

'It can also mean that you belong everywhere,'

said Somi. 'But you never told me. You are fair like a European.'

'I had not thought much about it.'

'Are you ashamed?'

'No. My guardian was. He kept it to himself, he only told me when I came home after playing Holi. I was happy then. So, when he told me, I was not ashamed, I was proud.'

'And now?'

'Now? Oh, I can't really believe it. Somehow I do not really feel mixed.'

'Then don't blame it for nothing.'

Rusty felt a little ashamed, and they were both silent awhile, then Somi shrugged and said, 'So you are going. You are running away from India.'

'No, not from India.'

'Then you are running away from your friends, from me!'

Rusty felt the irony of this remark, and allowed a tone of sarcasm into his voice.

'*You*, Master Somi, *you* are the one who is going away. I am still here. *You* are going to Amritsar. I only *want* to go. And I'm here alone; everyone has gone. So if I do eventually leave, the only person I'll be running away from will be myself!'

'Ah!' said Somi, nodding his head wisely. 'And by running away from yourself, you will be running away from me and from India! Now come on, let's go and have chaat.'

He pulled Rusty off the bed, and pushed him out of the room. Then, at the top of the steps, he leapt lightly on Rusty's back, kicked him with his heels, and shouted, 'Down the steps, my *tattoo,* my pony! Fast down the steps!'

So Rusty carried him downstairs and dropped him on the grass. They laughed, but there was no great joy in their laughter, they laughed for the sake of friendship.

'Best favourite friend,' said Somi, throwing a handful of mud in Rusty's face.

# The Lafunga

'If you have nothing to do,' said Devinder, 'will you come with me on my rounds?'

Rusty set out with Devinder in the direction of the bazaar. As it was early morning, the shops were just beginning to open. Vegetable vendors were busy freshening their stock with liberal sprinklings of water, calling their prices and their wares; children dawdled in the road on their way to school, playing hopscotch or marbles. Girls going to college chattered in groups like gay, noisy parrots. Men cycled to work, and bullock carts came in from the villages, laden with produce. The dust, which had taken all night to settle, rose again like a mist.

When they reached the Clock Tower, someone whistled to them from across the street, and a tall young man came striding towards them.

He looked taller than Devinder, mainly because of his long legs. He wore a loose-fitting bush-shirt that hung open in front. His face was long and pale, but he had quick, devilish eyes, and he smiled disarmingly.

---

Extract from *Vagrants in the Valley*

'Here comes Sudheer, the Lafunga,' whispered Devinder. 'Lafunga means loafer. He probably wants some money. He is the most charming and the most dangerous person in town.' Aloud, he said, 'Sudheer, when are you going to return the twenty rupees you owe me?'

'Don't talk that way, Devinder,' said the Lafunga, looking offended. 'Don't hurt my feelings. You know your money is safer with me than it is in the bank. It will even bring you dividends, mark my words. I have a plan that will come off in a few days, and then you will get back double your money. Please tell me, who is your friend?'

'We stay together,' said Devinder, introducing Rusty. 'And he is bankrupt too, so don't get any ideas.'

'Please don't believe what he says of me,' said the Lafunga with a captivating smile that showed his strong teeth. 'Really, I am not very harmful.'

'Well, completely harmless people are usually dull,' said Rusty.

'How I agree with you! I think we have a lot in common.' 'No, he hasn't got anything,' put in Devinder.

'Well then, he must start from the beginning. It is

the best way to make a fortune. You will come and see me, won't you, mister Rusty? We could make a terrific combination, I am sure. You are the kind of person people trust! They take only one look at me and then feel their pockets to see if anything is missing!'

Rusty instinctively put his hand to his own pocket, and all three of them laughed.

'Well, I must go,' said Sudheer, the Lafunga, now certain that Devinder was not likely to produce any funds. 'I have a small matter to attend to. It may bring me a fee of twenty or thirty rupees.'

'Go,' said Devinder. 'Strike while the iron is hot.'

'Not I,' said the Lafunga, grinning and moving off. 'I make the iron hot by striking.'

'Sudheer is not too bad,' said Devinder, as they walked away from the Clock Tower. 'He is a crook, of course—*Shree 420*—but he would not harm people like us. As he is quite well educated, he manages to gain the confidence of some well-to-do people, and acts on their behalf in matters that are not always respectable. But he spends what he makes, and is too generous to be successful.'

They had reached a quiet, tree-lined road, and walked in the shade of neem, mango, jamun and eucalyptus trees. Clumps of tall bamboo grew between the trees.

Some marigolds grew wild on the footpath, and Devinder picked two of them, giving one to Rusty.

'There is a girl who lives at the bottom of the road,' he said. 'She is a pretty girl. Come with me and see her.'

They walked to the house at the end of the road and, while Rusty stood at the gate, Devinder went up the path. Devinder stood at the bottom of the veranda steps, a little to one side, where he could be seen from a window, and whistled softly.

Presently, a girl came out on the veranda. When she saw Devinder, she smiled. She had a round, fresh face, and long black hair, and she was not wearing any shoes.

Devinder gave her the marigold. She took it in her hand and, not knowing what to say, ran indoors.

That morning, Devinder and Rusty walked about four miles. Devinder's customers ranged from decadent maharanis and the wives of government officials to gardeners and sweeper women. Though his merchandise was cheap, the well-to-do were more finicky about a price than the poor. And there were a few who bought things from Devinder because they knew his circumstances and liked what he was doing.

Returning to the bazaar, Devinder found Sudheer at a paan shop, his lips red with betel juice. Devinder went straight to the point.

'Sudheer,' he said, 'you owe me twenty rupees. I need it, not for myself, but for Rusty, who has to leave Dehra very urgently. You must get me the money by tonight.'

The Lafunga scratched his head.

'It will be difficult,' he said, 'but perhaps it can be managed. He really needs the money? It is not just a trick to get your own money back?'

'He is going to the hills. There may be money for him there, if he finds the person he is looking for.'

'Well, that's different,' said the Lafunga, brightening up. 'That makes Rusty an investment. Meet me at the Clock Tower at six o'clock, and I will have the money for you. I am glad to find you making useful friends for a change.'

He stuffed another roll of paan into his mouth,

and taking leave of Devinder with a bright red smile, strolled leisurely down the bazaar road.

As far as appearances went, he had little to do but loll around in the afternoon sunshine, frequenting tea shops, and gambling with cards in small back rooms. All this he did very well—but it did not earn him a living.

To say that he lived by his wits would be an exaggeration. He lived a great deal by other people's wits. There was the seth, for instance, Rusty's former landlord, who owned much property and dabbled in many shady transactions, and who was often represented by the Lafunga in affairs of an unsavoury nature.

Sudheer came originally from the Frontier, where little value was placed on human life. While still a boy, he had wandered, a homeless refugee, over the border into India. A smuggler adopted him, taught him something of the trade, and introduced him to some of the best hands in the profession; but in a border foray with the police, Sudheer's foster father was shot dead, and the youth was once again on his own. By this time he was old enough to look after himself. With the help of his foster father's connections, he soon secured the service and confidence of the seth.

Sudheer was no petty criminal. He practised crime as a fine art, and believed that thieves, and even murderers, had to have certain principles. If he stole, he stole from a rich man who could afford to be robbed, or from a greedy man who deserved to be robbed. And if he did not rob poor men, it was not because of any altruistic motive—it was because poor men were not worth robbing.

He was good to those friends, like Devinder, who were good to him. Perhaps his most valuable friends, as sources of both money and information, were the dancing girls who followed their profession in an almost inaccessible little road in the heart of the bazaar. His best friends were Hastini and Mrinalini. He borrowed money from them very freely, and seldom paid back more than half of it.

Hastini could twang the sitar, and dance—with a rather heavy tread—among various other accomplishments.

Mrinalini, a much smaller woman, had grown up in the profession. She was looked after by her mother, a former entertainer, who kept most of the money that Mrinalini made.

Sudheer woke Hastini in the middle of her

afternoon siesta by tickling her under the chin with a feather.

'And who were you with last night, little brother?' she asked running her fingers through his thick brown hair. 'You are smelling of some horrible perfume.'

'You know I do not spend my nights with anyone,' said Sudheer. 'The perfume is from yesterday.'

'Someone new?'

'No, my butterfly. I have known her for a week.'

'Too long a time,' said Hastini petulantly. 'A dangerously long time. How much have you spent on her?'

'Nothing so far. But that is not why I came to see you. Have you got twenty rupees?'

'Villain!' cried Hastini. 'Why do you always borrow from me when you want to entertain some stupid young thing? Are you so heartless?'

'My little lotus flower!' protested Sudheer, pinching her rosy cheeks. 'I am not borrowing for any such reason. A friend of mine has to leave Dehra urgently, and I must get the money for his train fare. I owe it to him.'

'Since when did you have a friend?'

'Never mind that. I have one. And I come to you for help because I love you more than any one else. Would you prefer that I borrow the money from Mrinalini?'

'You dare not,' said Hastini. 'I will kill you if you do.'

Between Hastini, of the broad hips, and Mrinalini, who was small and slender, there existed a healthy rivalry for the affections of Sudheer. Perhaps it was the great difference in their proportions that animated the rivalry. Mrinalini envied the luxuriousness of Hastini's soft body, while Hastini envied Mrinalini's delicacy, poise, slenderness of foot, and graceful walk. Mrinalini was the colour of milk and honey; she had the daintiness of a deer, while Hastini possessed the elegance of an elephant.

Sudheer could appreciate both these qualities.

He stood up, looking young even for his twenty-two years, and smiled a crooked smile. He might have looked effeminate had it not been for his hands—they were big, long-fingered, strong hands.

'Where is the money?' he asked.

'You are so impatient! Sit down, sit down. I have it here beneath the mattress.'

Sudheer's hand made its way beneath the mattress and probed about in search of the money.

'Ah, here it is! You have a fortune stacked away here. Yes, ten rupees, fifteen, twenty, and one for luck . . . Now give me a kiss!'

About an hour later Sudheer was in the street again, whistling cheerfully to himself. He walked with a long, loping stride, his shirt hanging open. Warm sunshine filled one side of the narrow street, and crept up the walls of shops and houses.

Sudheer passed a fruit stand, where the owner was busy talking to a customer, and helped himself to a choice red Kashmiri apple. He continued on his way down the bazaar road, munching the apple.

The bazaar continued for a mile, from the Clock Tower to the railway station, and Sudheer could hear the whistle of a train. He turned off at a little alley, throwing his half-eaten apple to a stray dog. Then he climbed a flight of stairs—wooden stairs that were loose and rickety, liable to collapse at any moment . . .

Mrinalini's half-deaf mother was squatting on the kitchen floor, lighting a fire in an earthen brazier. Sudheer poked his head round the door and shouted, 'Good morning, Mother, I hope you are making me some tea. You look fine today!' And then, in a lower tone, so that she could not hear: 'You look like a dried-up mango.'

'So it's you again,' grumbled the old woman. 'What do you want now?'

'Your most respectable daughter is what I want,' said Sudheer.

'What's that?' She cupped her hand to her ear and leaned forward.

'Where's Mrinalini?' shouted Sudheer.

'Don't shout like that! She is not here.'

'That's all I wanted to know,' said Sudheer, and he walked through the kitchen, through the living-room, and on to the veranda balcony, where he found Mrinalini sitting in the sun, combing out her long silken hair.

'Let me do it for you,' said Sudheer, and he took the comb from her hand and ran it through the silky black hair. 'For one so little, so much hair. You could conceal yourself in it, and not be seen, except for your dainty little feet.'

'What are you after, Sudheer? You are so full of compliments this morning. And watch out for Mother—if she sees you combing my hair, she will have a fit!'

'And I hope it kills her.'

'Sudheer!'

'Don't be so sentimental about your mother. You are her little gold mine, and she treats you as such—soon I will be having to fill in application forms before I can see you! It is time you kept your earnings for yourself.'

'So that it will be easier for you to help yourself?'

'Well, it would be more convenient. By the way, I have come to you for twenty rupees.'

Mrinalini laughed delightedly, and took the comb from Sudheer. 'What were you saying about my little feet?' she asked slyly.

'I said they were the feet of a princess, and I would be very happy to kiss them.'

'Kiss them, then.'

She held one delicate golden foot in the air, and Sudheer took it in his hands (which were as large as her feet) and kissed her ankles.

'That will be twenty rupees,' he said.

She pushed him away with her foot. 'But, Sudheer, I gave you fifteen rupees only three days ago. What have you done with it?' 'I haven't the slightest idea: I only know that I must have more. It is most urgent, you can be sure of that. But if you cannot help me, I must try elsewhere.'

'Do that, Sudheer. And may I ask, whom do you propose to try?'

'Well, I was thinking of Hastini.'

'*Who?*'

'You know, Hastini, the girl with the wonderful figure . . .'

'I should think I do! Sudheer, if you so much as dare to take a rupee from her, I'll never speak to you again!'

'Well, then, what shall I do?'

Mrinalini beat the arms of the chair with her little fists, and cursed Sudheer under her breath. Then she got up and went into the kitchen. A great deal of shouting went on in the kitchen before Mrinalini came back with flushed cheeks and fifteen rupees.

'You don't know the trouble I had getting it,' she said. 'Now don't come asking for more until at least a week has passed.' 'After a week, I will be able to supply you with funds. I am engaged tonight on a mission of some importance. In a few days I will place golden bangles on your golden feet.'

'What mission?' asked Mrinalini, looking at him

with an anxious frown. 'If it is anything to do with the seth, please leave it alone. You know what happened to Satish Dayal. He was smuggling opium for the seth, and now he is sitting in jail, while the seth continues as always.'

'Don't worry about me. I can deal with the seth.'

'Then be off! I have to entertain a foreign delegation this evening. You can come tomorrow morning, if you are free.'

'I may come. Meanwhile, goodbye!'

He walked backwards into the living room, pivoted into the kitchen and, bending over the old woman, kissed her on the forehead.

'You dried-up old mango,' he said. And went away, whistling.

# The Kitemaker

There was but one tree in the street known as Gali
Ram Nath—an ancient banyan that had grown
through the cracks of an abandoned mosque—and
little Ali's kite had caught in its branches. The boy,
barefoot and clad only in a torn shirt, ran along the
cobbled stones of the narrow street to where his
grandfather sat nodding dreamily in the sunshine of
their back courtyard.

'Grandfather,' shouted the boy. 'My kite has
gone!'

The old man woke from his daydream with a
start, and raising his head, displayed a beard that
would have been white, had it not been dyed red
with mehndi leaves.

'Did the twine break?' he asked. 'I know that
kite twine is not what it used to be.'

'No, grandfather, the kite is stuck in the banyan
tree.'

The old man chuckled. 'You have yet to learn
how to fly a kite properly, my child. And I am too
old to teach you, that's the pity of it. But you shall
have another.'

He had just finished making a new kite from

bamboo paper and thin silk, and it lay in the sun, firming up. It was a pale pink kite, with a small green tail. The old man handed it to Ali, and the boy raised himself on his toes and kissed his grandfather's hollowed-out cheek.

'I will not lose this one,' he said. 'This kite will fly like a bird.' And he turned on his heels and skipped out of the courtyard.

The old man remained dreaming in the sun. His kite shop was gone, the premises long since sold to a junk dealer; but he still made kites, for his own amusement and for the benefit of his grandson, Ali. Not many people bought kites these days. Adults disdained them, and children preferred to spend their money at the cinema. Moreover, there were not many open spaces left for the flying of kites. The city had swallowed up the open grassland that had stretched from the old fort's walls to the river bank.

But the old man remembered a time when grown men flew kites, and great battles were fought, the kites swerving and swooping in the sky, tangling with each other until the string of one was severed. Then the defeated but liberated kite would float away into the blue unknown. There was a good deal of betting, and money frequently changed hands.

Kite flying was then the sport of kings, and the

old man remembered how the Nawab himself would come down to the riverside with his retinue to participate in this noble pastime. There was time, then, to spend an idle hour with a gay, dancing strip of paper. Now, everyone hurried, hurried in a heat of hope, and delicate things like kites and daydreams were trampled underfoot.

He, Mehmood the kitemaker, had in the prime of his life been well-known throughout the city. Some of his more elaborate kites once sold for as much as three or four rupees each.

At the request of the Nawab he had once made a very special kind of kite, unlike any that had been seen in the district. It consisted of a series of small, very light paper disks, trailing on a thin bamboo frame. To the end of each disk he fixed a sprig of grass, forming a balance on both sides.

The surface of the foremost disk was slightly convex, and a fantastic face was painted on it, having two eyes made of small mirrors. The disks, decreasing in size from head to tail, assumed an undulatory form, and gave the kite the appearance of a crawling serpent. It required great skill to raise this cumbersome device from the ground, and only Mehmood could manage it.

Everyone had heard of the 'Dragon Kite' that Mehmood had built, and word went round that it possessed supernatural powers. A large crowd assembled in the open to watch its first public launching in the presence of the Nawab.

At the first attempt, it refused to leave the ground.

The disks made a plaintive, protesting sound, and the sun was trapped in the little mirrors, and made of the kite a living, complaining creature. And then the wind came from the right direction, and the Dragon Kite soared into the sky, wriggling its way higher and higher, with the sun still glinting in its devil eyes. And when it went very high, it pulled fiercely on the twine, and Mehmood's young sons had to help him with the reel; but still the kite pulled, determined to be free, to break loose, to live a life of its own. And eventually it did so.

The twine snapped, the kite leaped away towards the sun, sailed on heavenward until it was lost to view. It was never found again, and Mehmood wondered afterwards if he had made too vivid, too living a thing of the great kite. He did not make another like it, and instead he presented to the Nawab a musical kite, one that made a sound like a violin when it rose in the air.

Those were more leisurely, more spacious days. But the Nawab had died years ago, and his descendants were almost as poor as Mehmood himself. Kitemakers, like poets, once had their patrons; but no one knew Mehmood, simply because there were too many people in the gali, and they could not be bothered with their neighbours.

When Mehmood was younger and had fallen sick, everyone in the neighbourhood had come to ask after his health; but now, when his days were drawing to a close, no one visited him. True, most of his old friends were dead and his sons had grown up: one was working in a local garage, the other had been in Pakistan at the time of Partition and had not been able to rejoin his relatives.

The children who had bought kites from him ten years ago were now grown men, struggling for a living; they did not have time for the old man and his memories. They had grown up in a swiftly changing and competitive world, and they looked at the old kitemaker and the banyan tree with the same indifference.

Both were taken for granted—permanent fixtures that were of no concern to the raucous, sweating mass of humanity that surrounded them. No longer did people gather under the banyan tree to discuss their problems and their plans: only in the summer months did a few seek shelter from the fierce sun.

But there was the boy, his grandson; it was good that Mehmood's son worked close by, for it gladdened the old man's heart to watch the small boy at play in the winter sunshine, growing under his eyes like a young and well-nourished sapling putting forth new leaves each day. There is a great affinity between trees and men. We grow at much the same pace, if we are not hurt or starved or cut down. In our youth we are resplendent creatures, and in our declining years we stoop a little, we remember, we stretch our brittle limbs in the sun, and then, with a sigh, we shed our last leaves.

Mehmood was like the banyan, his hands gnarled and twisted like the roots of the ancient tree. Ali was like the young mimosa planted at the end of the courtyard. In two years both he and the tree would acquire the strength and confidence of their early youth.

The voices in the street grew fainter, and Mehmood wondered if he was going to fall asleep and dream, as he so often did, of a kite so beautiful and powerful that it would resemble the great white bird of the Hindus, Garuda, God Vishnu's famous steed. He would like to make a wonderful new kite for little Ali. He had nothing else to leave the boy.

He heard Ali's voice in the distance, but did not realize that the boy was calling him. The voice seemed to come from very far away.

Ali was at the courtyard door, asking if his mother had as yet returned from the bazaar. When Mehmood did not answer, the boy came forward repeating his question. The sunlight was slanting across the old man's head, and a small white butterfly rested on his flowing beard. Mehmood was silent; and when Ali put his small brown hand on the old man's shoulder, he met with no response. The boy heard a faint sound, like the rubbing of marbles in his pocket.

Suddenly afraid, Ali turned and moved to the door, and then ran down the street shouting for his mother. The butterfly left the old man's beard and flew to the mimosa tree, and a sudden gust of wind caught the torn kite and lifted it into the air, carrying it far above the struggling city into the blind blue sky.

# The Box Man

Sitting outside my cottage, in the summer shade of an old plum tree, I can see a path leading through the deodars towards the next tree-darkened mountain. On this morning, I saw an old man coming down the path, walking very slowly, carrying a small tin trunk on his head.

He stopped at the gate and asked me if I would buy something. I could think of nothing I wanted, but the old man looked so tired, so very old, that I thought he would collapse if he moved any further along the path without resting. So I asked him to step in and show me his wares. He had a snow-white beard, crinkled brown skin, and bright intelligent eyes. He was thin and bandy-legged and wore a patched, black waistcoat.

He couldn't get the box off his head by himself, but together we managed to set it down in the shade and the old man insisted on spreading the entire contents out on the grass: bangles, combs, shoelaces, safety pins, cheap stationery, buttons, pomades, elastic, and scores of other minor household necessities.

When I refused buttons because there was no

one to sew them on for me, he plied me with safety
pins. I said no; but, as he moved from article to
article, his querulous, persuasive voice slowly broke
down my sales resistance, and I ended up buying
envelopes, a letter pad (pink roses on bright blue
paper), a one-rupee fountain pen, and several yards
of elastic. I had no idea what I would use the elastic
for, but the old man convinced me that I could no
longer live without it.

He then produced a small plastic glass from his
waistcoat pocket, and I thought it was another item
for sale. But he only wanted a drink of water. I
readily brought him some. He drank the water
slowly, then leant back against the trunk of the
plum tree, making no effort to pack his things. He
closed his eyes. I had a sudden panicky feeling that
he would die in my garden!

'I am very tired, hazoor,' he said. 'Please do not
mind if I rest here for a while.' 'Rest for as long as
you like,' I said. 'That's a heavy load to carry on a
hot day.' He opened his eyes at the chance of a
conversation and said, 'When I was a young man, it
was nothing. I could carry my box up from Rajpur
to Mussoorie by the bridle path—seven steep miles!
But now I find it difficult to cover even one mile

from the bazaar to the Mall.'

'Naturally, you are old.' 'Seventy years old, sahib.' 'You are very fit for your age. You do not look more than sixty-five.' Though he was frail, he had a wiry frame and his skin still had a healthy colour. 'Don't you have anyone to help you?' I asked.

'I had a boy last month, but he stole my earnings and ran off to *Dilli*. I wish my son was alive—he would not have permitted me to work like a mule for a living. But he died five years ago, of a cough.' By a 'cough', I presume, he meant tuberculosis. 'Have you no relatives, then?' 'None. I have outlived them all. That is the curse of a healthy life. Your friends, your loved ones, all go before you, and at the end you are left alone. But I must go too, before long. The road seems more difficult each day. I feel as though it has added a mile to its length. The stones are harder. The sun is hotter. Even some of the trees that were here in my youth have grown old and died. I have outlived the trees.'

He had outlived the trees. And I was certain that if he fell asleep in my garden, he would strike root there, sending out crooked branches. I could imagine a small bent tree with a black waistcoat. He closed his eyes again, but kept on talking.

'Yes, there were times when the memsahibs bought great quantities of elastic. Today, it is ribbons and bangles for the girls, and combs for the boys. But I do not make so much. Not because people do not buy from me, but because I cannot walk as far. How many houses do I reach in a day? Ten, fifteen. But twenty years ago I could walk to fifty houses. That makes a difference.'

'Have you always been here?'

'Most of my life, hazoor. Except when I went to Najibabad to get married. I was here before they built the motor road, when gentlemen came up on ponies, and their women in dandies borne by coolies. I was here when the Prince of *Welles* came from across the sea. And I was here during the earthquake—when that was, I cannot remember exactly, I was only a boy—but the hills shook and many houses fell. Oh, I have been here a long time, hazoor. I was here when this house was built. Fifty, sixty years ago, it must have been. I cannot remember exactly. What is ten years when you have lived seventy? It was a Major Sahib who built your house. I remember, because he did not live in it for long. He was thrown from his horse one day, and was killed. Then came—I forget the name—and his wife and children. Beautiful children. But they went away many years ago. Everyone has gone away.'

'But others have come,' I said. 'True, and that is as it should be. That is not my complaint. My complaint is that I have been left behind.' He produced his little glass again. 'I am sorry, hazoor, but talking has made me thirsty.'

I took the glass and went indoors to fill it. By the time I returned to the garden, the old man had miraculously put away all his odds and ends. He stood over his old blue tin box, gazing down at it with a mixture of disdain and affection.

I helped him lift it, and placed it on the flattened cloth on his head. I opened the gate, and the box man tottered out. He did not have the energy to turn and make a salutation of any kind; but, setting his sights on the mountain ahead, he walked up the path with steps that were shaky and slow but wonderfully straight.

I watched him until he was far along the path. I wondered how long he could last. Perhaps a year or two, perhaps a day, perhaps an hour. But whenever or however he died, it wouldn't be death.

He was too old to die. He could only sleep. He could only fall gently, like an old brown leaf.

# Pipalnagar's People

*One*

'Look, Ganpat,' I said one day, 'I've heard a lot of stories about you, and I don't know which is true. How did you get your crooked back?'

'That's a very long story,' he said, flattered by my interest in him. 'And I don't know if you will believe it. Besides, it is not to anyone that I would speak freely.'

He had served his purpose in whetting my appetite. I said, 'I'll give you four annas if you tell me your story. How about that?' He stroked his beard, considering my offer. 'All right,' he said, squatting down on his haunches in the sunshine, while I pulled myself up on a low wall. 'But it happened more than twenty years ago, and you cannot expect me to remember very clearly.'

In those days (said Ganpat) I was quite a young man, and had just been married. I owned several acres of land and, though we were not rich, we were

---

Extract from *Delhi Is Not Far*

^

not very poor. When I took my produce to the market, five miles away, I harnessed the bullocks and drove down the dusty village road. I would return home at night.

Every night, I passed a peepul tree, and it was said this tree was haunted. I had never met the ghost and did not believe in him, but his name, I was told, was Bippin, and long ago he had been hanged on the peepul tree by a band of dacoits. Ever since, his ghost had lived in the tree, and was in the habit of pouncing upon any person who resembled a dacoit, and beating him severely. I suppose I must have looked dishonest, for one night Bippin decided to pounce on me. He leapt out of the tree and stood in the middle of the road, blocking the way.

'You, there!' he shouted. 'Get off your cart. I am going to kill you!'

I was, of course, taken aback, but saw no reason why I should obey.

'I have no intention of being killed,' I said. 'Get on the cart yourself!'

'Spoken like a man!' cried Bippin, and he jumped up on the cart beside me. 'But tell me one good reason why I should not kill you?'

'I am not a dacoit,' I replied.

'But you look like one. That is the same thing.'

'You would be sorry for it later if you killed me. I am a poor man with a wife to support.'

'You have no reason for being poor,' said Bippin, angrily.

'Well, make me rich if you can.'

'So you think I don't have the power to make you rich? Do you defy me to make you rich?'

'Yes,' I said, 'I defy you to make me rich.'

'Then drive on!' cried Bippin. 'I am coming home with you.' I drove the bullock cart into the village, with Bippin sitting beside me.

'I have so arranged it,' he said, 'that no one but you will be able to see me. And another thing. I must sleep beside you every night, and no one must know of it. If you tell anyone about me, I'll kill you immediately!'

'Don't worry,' I said. 'I won't tell anyone.'

'Good. I look forward to living with you. It was getting lonely in that peepul tree.'

So Bippin came to live with me, and he slept beside me every night, and we got on very well together. He was as good as his word, and money began to pour in from every conceivable and inconceivable source, until I was in a position to buy more land and cattle. Nobody knew of our association, though of course my friends and relatives wondered where all the money was coming from. At the same time, my wife was rather upset at my refusing to sleep with her at night. I could not very well keep her in the same bed as a ghost, and Bippin was most particular about sleeping beside me. At first, I had told my wife I wasn't well, that I would sleep on the veranda. Then I told her that there was someone after our cows, and I would have to keep an eye on them at night. Bippin and I slept in the barn.

My wife would often spy on me at night, suspecting infidelity, but she always found me lying alone with the cows. Unable to understand my strange behaviour, she mentioned it to her family. They came to me, demanding an explanation.

At the same time, my own relatives were insisting that I tell them the source of my increasing income. Uncles and aunts and distant cousins all descended on me one day, wanting to know where the money was coming from.

'Do you want me to die?' I said, losing patience with them. 'If I tell you the cause of my wealth, I will surely die.'

But they laughed, taking this for a half-hearted excuse. They suspected I was trying to keep everything for myself. My wife's relatives insisted that I had found another woman. Eventually, I grew so exhausted with their demands that I blurted out the truth.

They didn't believe the truth either (who does?), but it gave them something to think and talk about, and they went away for the time being.

But that night, Bippin didn't come to sleep beside me. I was all alone with the cows. And he didn't come the following night. I had been afraid he would kill me while I slept, but it appeared that he had gone his way and left me to my own devices. I was certain that my good fortune had come to an end, and so I went back to sleeping with my wife.

The next time I was driving back to the village from the market, Bippin leapt out of the peepul tree.

'False friend!' he cried, halting the bullocks. 'I gave you everything you wanted, and still you betrayed me!'

'I'm sorry,' I said. 'You can kill me if you like.'

'No, I cannot kill you,' he said. 'We have been friends for too long. But I will punish you all the same.'

Picking up a stout stick, he struck me three times across the back, until I was bent up double.

'After that,' Ganpat concluded, 'I could never straighten up again and, for over twenty years, I have been a crooked man. My wife left me and went back to her family, and I could no longer work in the fields. I left my village and wandered from one city to another, begging for a living. That is how I came to Pipalnagar, where I decided to remain. People here seem to be more generous than they are in other towns, perhaps because they haven't got so much.'

He looked up at me with a smile, waiting for me to produce the four annas.

'You can't expect me to believe that story,' I said. 'But it was a good invention, so here is your money.'

'No, no!' said Ganpat, backing away and affecting indignation. 'If you don't believe me, keep the money. I would not lie to you for a mere four annas!'

He permitted me to force the coin into his hand, and then went hobbling away, having first wished me a pleasant afternoon.

I was almost certain he had been telling me a very tall story; but you never can tell . . . Perhaps he really had met Bippin the ghost. And it was wise to give him the four annas, just in case, after all, he was a CID man.

## Two

Pitamber is a young lion. A shaggy mane of black hair tumbles down the nape of his neck. His body, though, is naked and hairless, burnt a rich chocolate by the summer sun. His only garment is a pair of knickers. When he pedals his cycle-rickshaw through the streets of Pipalnagar, the muscles of his calves and thighs stand out like lumps of grey iron. He has carried in his rickshaw fat baniyas and their fat wives, and this has given him powerful legs, a strong back and hollow cheeks. His thighs are magnificent, solid muscle, not an ounce of surplus flesh. They look as though they have been carved out of teak.

His face, though, is gaunt and hollow, his eyes set deep in their sockets. But there is a burning intensity about his eyes and sometimes I wonder if he, too, is tubercular, like many in Pipalnagar. You cannot tell just by looking at a person if he is sick. Sometimes the weak will last for years, while the strong will suddenly collapse and die.

Pitamber has a wife and three children in his
village five miles from Pipalnagar. They have a few
acres of land on which they grow maize and
sugarcane. One day he made me sit in his rickshaw,
and we cycled out of the town, along the road to
Delhi. Then we had to get down and push the
rickshaw over a rutted cart-track, until we reached
his village.

This visit to Pitamber's village had provided me
with an escape route from Pipalnagar. I persuaded
Suraj to put aside his tray and his books, and hiring
a cycle from a stand near the bus stop (on credit), I
seated Suraj in front of me on the crossbar, and rode
out of Pipalnagar.

It was then that I made the amazing discovery
that by exerting my legs a little, I could get out of
Pipalnagar, and that, except for the cycle-hire, it did
not involve any expense or great sacrifice.

It was a hot, sunny morning, and I was
perspiring by the time we had gone two miles; but a
fresh wind sprang up suddenly, and I could smell
rain in the air, though there were no clouds to be
seen.

When Suraj began to feel cramped on the
saddle-bar, we got down, and walked along the side

of the road.

'Let us not go to the village,' said Suraj. 'Let us go where there are no people at all. I am tired of people.'

We pushed the cycle off the road, and took a path through a paddy field, and then a field of young maize, and in the distance we saw a tree, a crooked tree, growing beside a well.

I do not know the name of that tree. I had never seen one of its kind before. It had a crooked trunk, and crooked branches, and it was clothed in thick, broad crooked leaves, like the leaves on which food is served in the bazaars.

In the trunk of the tree was a hole, and when I set my cycle down with a crash, two green parrots flew out of the hole, and went dipping and swerving across the fields.

There was grass around the well, cropped short by grazing cattle, so we sat in the shade of the crooked tree, and Suraj untied the red cloth in which he had brought our food.

We ate our bread and spiced vegetables, and meanwhile the parrots returned to the tree.

'Let us come here every week,' said Suraj, stretching himself out on the grass and resting his head against my shoulder.

It was a drowsy day, the air humid, and soon Suraj fall asleep. I, too, stretched myself out on the grass, and closed my eyes but I did not sleep. I was aware instead of a score of different sensations.

I heard a cricket singing in the crooked tree; the cooing of pigeons which dwelt in the walls of the old well; the quiet breathing of Suraj; a rustling in the leaves of the tree; the distant hum of an aeroplane.

I smelt the grass, and the old bricks round the well and the promise of rain.

I felt Suraj's fingers touching my arm, and the sun creeping over my cheek.

I opened my eyes, and I saw the clouds on the horizon, and Suraj still asleep, his arm thrown across his eyes to keep away the glare.

Being thirsty, I went to the well, and putting my shoulders to it, turned the wheel, walking around the well four times, while cool, clean water gushed out over the stones and along the channel to the fields.

I drank from one of the trays and the water was sweet with age.

Suraj was sitting up, looking at the sky.

'It is going to rain,' he said. When he had taken

his fill of water, we pushed the cycle back to the main road and began cycling homewards, but we were still two miles out of Pipalnagar when it began to rain.

A lashing wind swept the rain across our faces, but we exulted in it, and sang at the top of our voices until we reached the bus stop. I left the cycle at the hire-shop. Suraj and I ran up the rickety, swaying steps to my room.

Soon there were puddles on the floor, where we had left our soaking clothes, and Suraj was sitting on the bed, a sheet wrapped round his chest.

He became feverish that evening, and I pulled out an old blanket, and covered him with it. I massaged his scalp with mustard oil, and he fell asleep while I did this.

It was dark by then, and the rain had stopped, and the bazaar was lighting up. I curled up at the foot of the bed, and slept for a little while; but at midnight I was woken by the moon shining full in my face; a full moon, shedding its light exclusively on Pipalnagar and peeping and prying into every room, washing the empty streets, silvering the corrugated tin roof.

People are restless tonight, with the moon

shining through their windows. Suraj turns
restlessly in his sleep. Kamla, having sent away a
drunken customer, will be bathing herself, as she
always does before she finally sleeps . . . Deep
Chand is tossing on his cot, dreaming of electric
razors and a plush hair-cutting saloon in the capital,
with the Prime Minister as his client. And Seth
Govind Ram, unable to sleep because of the
accusing moonlight, paces his veranda, worrying
about his rent, counting up his assets, and
wondering if he should stand for election to the
Legislative Assembly.

In the temple the moonlight rests gently on the
generous Ganesh, and in the fields Krishna is
playing his flute and Radha is singing . . . 'I follow
you, devoted . . . How can you deceive me, so
tortured by love's fever as I am . . .'

*Three*
In June, the lizards hang listlessly on the walls,
scanning their horizon in vain. Insects seldom show
up—either the heat has killed them, or they are
sleeping and breeding in cracks in the plaster. The
lizards wait—and wait . . .

All Pipalnagar is waiting for its release from the

oppressive heat of June.

One day clouds loom up on the horizon, growing rapidly into enormous towers. A faint breeze springs up. Soon it is a wind, which brings with it the first raindrops. This is the moment everyone is waiting for. People run out of their chawls and houses to take in the fresh breeze and the scent of those first raindrops on the parched, dusty earth . . .

As most of my writing is done at night, and much of my sleeping by day, it often happens that at about midnight I put down my pen and go out for a walk. In Pipalnagar, this is a pleasant time for a walk, provided you are not taken for a burglar. There is the smell of jasmine in the air, the moonlight shining on sandy stretches of wasteland, and a silence broken only by the hideous bellow of the chowkidar, or night-watchman.

This is the person who, employed by the residents of our Mohalla, keeps guard over us at night, and walks the roads calling like a jackal, 'Khabardar!'(Beware) for the benefit of prospective evil-doers. Apart from keeping half the population awake, he is successful in warning thieves of his presence.

The other night, in the course of a midnight stroll, I encountered our chowkidar near a dark corner, and wished him a good evening. He leapt into the air like a startled rabbit, and immediately shouted 'Khabardar!' as though this was some magic word that would bring me down on my knees begging for mercy.

'It's quite all right,' I assured him. 'I'm only one of your clients.'

The chowkidar laughed nervously and said he was glad to hear it; he hoped I didn't mind his shouting 'Khabardar' at me, but these were grim times and robbers were on the increase.

I said yes, there were probably quite a few of them at work this very night. Had he ever tried creeping up on them quietly? He might catch a few that way.

But why should he catch them, the chowkidar wanted to know. It was his business to frighten them away. He could do that better by roaring defiantly on the roads than by accosting them on someone's premises—violence must be avoided, if he could help it.

'Besides,' he said, 'the people who live here like

me to shout at night. It makes them feel safe, knowing that I am on guard. And if I didn't shout "Khabardar" every few minutes, they would think I had fallen asleep, and I would be dismissed.'

This was a logical argument. I asked him what would he do if, by accident, he encountered a gang of thieves. He said he would keep shouting 'Khabardar' until the people came out of their houses to help him. I said I doubted very much if they would come out of their houses, but wished him luck all the same, and continued with my walk.

Every five minutes or so I heard his cry, followed by a 'Khabardar' which grew fainter until the chowkidar had reached the far side of the Mohalla. I thought it would be a good idea to give him a helping hand from my side, so I cupped my hands to my mouth and shouted, 'Khabardar, Khabardar!'

It worked like magic.

Three dark figures scrambled over a neighbouring wall and fled down the empty road. I shouted 'Khabardar' a second time, and they ran faster. Imagine the thieves' confusion when they were met by more 'Khabardars' in front, coming from the chowkidar, and realized that there were now two chowkidars operating in the Mohalla.

On those nights when sleep was elusive we left the room and walked for miles around Pipalnagar. It was generally about midnight that we became restless. The walls of the room would give out all the heat they had absorbed during the day, and to lie awake sweating in the dark only gave rise to morbid and depressing thoughts.

In our singlets and pyjamas Suraj and I would walk barefooted through the empty Mohalla, over the cooling brick pavements, until we were out of the bazaar and crossing the Maidan, our feet sinking into the springy dew-fresh grass. The Maidan was broad and spacious, and the star swept sky seemed to meet each end of the plain.

Then out of the town, through lantana scrub, till we came to the dry river bed, where we walked amongst rocks and boulders, sitting down occasionally, while great horny lizards watched us from between the stones.

Across the river bed fields of maize stretched away for a few miles, until there came a dry region, where thorns and a few bent trees grew, the earth splitting up in jagged cracks like a jigsaw puzzle; and where water had been, the skin was peeling off the earth in great flat pancakes. Dotting the landscape were old abandoned brick kilns, and it was said that thieves met there at nights, in the trenches around the kilns; but we never saw any.

When it rained heavily, the hollows filled up with water. Suraj and I came to one of these places to bathe and swim. There was an island in the middle of one of the hollows, and on this small mound stood the ruins of a hut, where a night-watchman once lived and looked after the bricks at night.

We swam out to the island, which was only a few yards away. There was a grassy patch in front of the hut, and here we lay and sunned ourselves in the early morning, until it became too hot. We would oil and massage each other's bodies, and wrestle on the grass.

Though I was heavier than Suraj, and my chest was as sound as a new drum, he had a lot of power in his long arms and legs and often pinioned me about the waist with his bony knees or fastened me with his strong fingers.

Once while we wrestled on the new monsoon grass, I felt his body go tense, as I strained to press his back to the ground. He stiffened, his thigh jerked against me, and his legs began to twitch. I knew that he had a fit coming on, but I was unable to extricate myself from his arms, which gripped me more tightly as the fit took possession of him. Instead of struggling, I lay still, and tried desperately to absorb some of his anguish by embracing him. I felt my own body might draw some of the agitation to itself; it was only a strange fancy, but I felt that it made a difference, that by consciously sharing his unconscious condition I was alleviating it. At other times, I have known this same feeling. When Kamla was burning with fever, I had thought that by taking her in my arms I could draw the fever from her, absorb the heat of her body, transfer to hers the coolness of my own.

Now I pressed against Suraj, and whispered soothingly and lovingly into his ear, though I knew he had no idea what I could be saying. And then when I noticed his mouth working, I thrust my hand in sideways to prevent him from biting his tongue.

But so violent was the convulsion that his teeth bit into the flesh of my palm and ground against my knuckles. I gasped with pain and tried to jerk my hand away, but it was impossible to loosen the grip of his teeth. So I closed my eyes and counted one, two, three, four, five, six, seven—until I felt his body relax again and his jaws give way slowly.

My hand had blood on it, and was trembling. I bound it in a handkerchief before Suraj came to himself.

We walked back to the town without talking much. He looked depressed and hopeless, though I knew he would be buoyant again before long. I kept my hand concealed beneath my singlet, and he was too dejected to notice this. It was only at night, when he returned from his classes, that he noticed it was bandaged, and then I told him I had slipped on the road, cutting my hand on some broken glass.

*Four*

Rain upon Pipalnagar: and until the rain stops, Pipalnagar is fresh and clean and alive. The children run out of their houses, glorying in their nakedness. They are innocent and unashamed. Older children, by no means innocent, but by all means unashamed, romp through the town, inviting the shocked disapproval of their elders and, presumably, betters.

Before we are ten, we are naked and free and unafraid; after ten, we must cloak our manhood, for we are no longer certain that we are men.

The gutters choke, and the Mohalla becomes a

mountain stream, coursing merrily down towards
the bus stop. And it is at the bus stop that
pandemonium breaks loose; for newly-arrived
passengers panic at the sight of the sea of mud and
rainwater that surrounds them on all sides, and
about a hundred tongas and cycle-rickshaws try all
at once to take care of a score of passengers. Result:
only half the passengers find a conveyance, while
the other half find themselves knee-deep in
Pipalnagar mire.

Pitamber has, of course, succeeded in acquiring
as his passenger the most attractive and frightened
young woman in the bus. He proceeds to show off
his skill and daring by taking her home by the most
devious and uncomfortable route, and when she
gets her feet covered with mud, wipes them with the
seedy red cloth that he ties about his neck.

The rain swirls over the trees and roofs of the
town, and the parched earth soaks it up, exuding a
fragrance that comes only once in a year, the
fragrance of quenched earth, the most exhilarating
of all smells.

And in my room, too, I am battling against the
elements, for the door will not shut against the
breeze, and the rain is sweeping in through the

opening and soaking my cot.

When, eventually, I succeed in barricading the floor, I find the roof leaking, and the water trickling down the walls, obliterating the dusty designs I have made on the plaster with my foot. I place a tin here and a mug there, and then, satisfied that everything is under control, sit on my cot and watch the roof-tops through my window.

But there is a loud banging on the door. It flies open with the pressure, and there is Suraj, standing on the threshold, shaking himself like a wet dog. Coming in, he strips off all his clothes, and then he dries himself with a torn threadbare towel, and sits shivering on the bed while I make frantic efforts to close the door again.

'You are cold, Suraj, I will make you some tea.'

He nods, forgetting to smile for once, and I know his mind is elsewhere, in one of a thousand places and all of them dreams.

When I have got the fire going, and placed the kettle on the red hot coals, I sit down beside Suraj and put my arm around his bony shoulders and dream a little with him.

'One day I will write a book,' I tell him. 'Not a murder story, but a real book, about real people.

Perhaps it will be about you and me and Pipalnagar.
And then we will break away from Pipalnagar, fly
away like eagles, and our troubles will be over and
fresh new troubles will begin. I do not mind
difficulties, as long as they are new difficulties.'

'First I must pass my exams,' said Suraj.
'Without a certificate one can do nothing, go
nowhere.'

'Who taught you such nonsense? While you are
preparing for your exams, I will be writing my
book. That's it! I will start tonight. It is an
auspicious night, the first night of the monsoon. Let
us start tonight.'

And by the time we had drunk our tea it was
evening and growing dark. The light did not come
on; a tree must have fallen across the wires. So I lit a
candle and placed it on the window sill (the rain and
wind had ceased). While the candle spluttered in the
steady stillness, Suraj opened his books and with
one hand on a book, and the other playing with his
toes—this helped him to read—he began his studies.

I took the ink down from the shelf, and finding
the bottle empty, added a little rainwater to it from
one of the mugs. I sat down beside Suraj and began
to write; but the pen was no good, and made

blotches all over and I didn't really know what to write about, though I was full of writing just then.

So I began to look at Suraj instead; at his eyes, hidden in the shadows, his hands in the candle light; and felt his breathing and the slight movement of his lips as he read softly to himself.

A gust of wind came through the window, and the candle went out. I swore softly in Punjabi.

'Never mind,' said Suraj, 'I was tired of reading.'

'But I was writing.'

'Your book?'

'No, a letter . . .'

'I have never known you to write letters, except to publishers asking them for money. To whom were you writing?'

'To you,' I said. 'And I will send you the letter one day, perhaps when we are no longer together.'

'I will wait for it, then. I will not read it now.'

*Five*

At ten o'clock on a wet night Pipalnagar had its first earthquake in thirty years. It lasted exactly five seconds. A low, ominous rumble was followed by a few quick shudders, and the water surahi jumped off the window ledge and crashed on the floor.

By the time Suraj and I had tumbled out of the room, the shock was over; but panic prevailed, and the entire population of the Mohalla was out in the street. One old man of seventy leapt from a first floor balcony and broke his neck; a large crowd had gathered round his body. Several women had fainted. On the other hand, many were shrieking and running about. Only a few days back astrologers had predicted the end of the world, and everyone was convinced that this was only the first of a series of earthquakes.

At temples and other places of worship prayer meetings were held. People moved about the street, pointing out the cracks that had appeared in their houses. Some of these cracks had, of course, been there for years, and were only now being discovered.

At midnight, men and women were still about; and, as though to justify their prudence, another, milder tremor made itself felt. The roof of an old house, weakened by many heavy monsoons, was encouraged to give way, and fell with a suitably awe-inspiring crash. Fortunately, no one was beneath it. Everyone was soaking wet by now, as the rain had come down harder, but no one dared venture indoors, specially after a roof had fallen in.

Worse still, the electricity failed and the entire Mohalla plunged into darkness. People huddled together, fearing the worst, while the rain came down incessantly.

'More people will die of pneumonia than earthquake,' observed Suraj. 'Let's go for a walk, it is better than standing about doing nothing.'

We rolled up our pyjamas and went splashing through the puddles. On the outskirts of the town we met Pitamber dancing in the middle of the road. He was very merry, and quite drunk.

'Why are you dancing in the road?' I asked.

'Because I am happy, that's why,' said Pitamber.

'And what makes you so happy, my friend?'

'Because I am dancing in the road,' he replied.

We began walking home again. The rain had stopped. There was a break in the clouds and a pale moon appeared. The neem trees gave out a strong, sweet smell.

There were no more tremors that night. When we got back to the Mohalla, the sky was lighter, and people were beginning to move into their houses again.

We lay on our island, in the shade of a thorn bush, watching a pair of sarus cranes on the opposite bank prancing and capering around each other. Tall, stork-like birds, with naked red heads and long red legs.

'We might be saruses in some future life,' I said.

'I hope so,' said Suraj. 'Even if it means being born on a lower level. I would like to be a beautiful white bird. I am tired of being a man, but I do not want to leave the world altogether. It is very lovely, sometimes.'

'I would like to be a sacred bird,' I said. 'I don't wish to be shot at.'

'Aren't saruses sacred? Look how they enjoy themselves.'

'They are making love. That is their principal occupation apart from feeding themselves. And they are so devoted to each other that if one bird is killed, the other will haunt the scene for weeks, calling distractedly. They have even been known to pine away and die of grief. That's why they are held in such affection by people in villages.'

'So many birds are sacred.'

We saw a bluejay swoop down from a tree—a flash of blue—and carry off a grasshopper.

Both the bluejay and Lord Siva are called Nilkanth. Siva has a blue throat, like the bluejay, because out of compassion for the human race he swallowed a deadly poison which was meant to destroy the world. He kept the poison in his throat and would not let it go any further.

'Are squirrels sacred?' asked Suraj, curiously watching one fumbling with a piece of bread which we had thrown away.

'Krishna loved them. He would take them in his arms and stroke them with his long, gentle fingers. That is why they have four dark lines down their backs from head to tail. Krishna was very dark skinned, and the lines are the marks of his fingers.'

'We should be gentle to animals . . . Why do we kill so many of them?'

'It is not so important that we do not kill them—it is important that we respect them. We must acknowledge their right to live on this earth. Everywhere, birds and animals are finding it more difficult to survive, because we are destroying their homes. They have to keep moving as the trees and the green grass keep disappearing.'

Flowers in Pipalnagar—do they exist?

I have known flowers in poetry, and as a child I knew a garden in Lucknow where there were fields of flowers, and another garden where only roses grew. In the fields round Pipalnagar I have seen dandelions that evaporate when you breathe on them, and sometimes a yellow buttercup nestling among thistles. But in our Mohalla, there are no flowers except one. This is a marigold growing out of a crack in my balcony.

I have removed the plaster from the base of the plant, and filled in a little earth which I water every morning. The plant is healthy, and sometimes it produces a little orange marigold, which I pluck and give away before it dies.

Sometimes Suraj keeps the flower in his tray, among the combs and scent bottles and buttons that he sells. Sometimes he offers the flower to a passing child—to a girl who runs away; or it might be a boy who tears the flower to shreds. Some children keep it; others give flowers to Suraj when he passes their houses.

Suraj has a flute which he plays whenever he is tired of going from house to house.

He will sit beneath a shady banyan or peepul, put his tray aside, and take out his flute. The haunting little notes travel down the road in the afternoon stillness, and children come to sit beside him and listen to the flute music. They are very quiet when he plays, because there is a little sadness about his music, and children specially can sense that sadness.

Suraj has made flutes cut of pieces of bamboo; but he never sells them, he gives them away to the children he likes. He will sell anything, but not his flutes.

Sometimes Suraj plays his flute at night, when I am lying awake on the cot, unable to sleep; and even when I fall asleep, the flute is playing in my dreams. Sometimes he brings it with him to the crooked tree, and plays it for the benefit of the birds; but the parrots only make harsh noises and fly away.

Once, when Suraj was playing his flute to a group of children, he had a fit. The flute fell from his hands, and he began to roll about in the dust on the roadside. The children were frightened and ran away.

But they did not stay away for long. The next time they heard the flute play, they came to listen as usual.

*Six*

As Suraj and I walked over a hill near the limestone quarries, past the shacks of the Rajasthani labourers, we met a funeral procession on its way to the cremation ground. Suraj placed his hand on my arm and asked me to wait until the procession had passed. At the same time a cyclist dismounted and stood at the side of the road. Others hurried on, without glancing at the little procession.

'I was taught to respect the dead in this way,' said Suraj. 'Even if you do not respect a man in life, you should respect him in death. The body is unimportant, but we should honour it out of respect for the man's mind.'

'It is a good custom,' I said.

'It must be difficult to live on after one you have loved has died.'

'I don't know. It has not happened to me. If a love is strong, I cannot see its end . . . It cannot end in death, I feel . . . Even physically, you would exist for me somehow.'

He was asleep when I returned late at night from a card game in which I had lost fifty rupees. I was a little drunk, and when I tripped near the doorway, he woke up; and though he did not open his eyes, I felt he was looking at me.

I felt very guilty and ashamed, because he had been ill that day, and I had forgotten it. Now there was no point in saying I was sorry. Drunkenness is really a vice, because it degrades a man, and humiliates him.

Prostitution is degrading, but a prostitute can still keep her dignity; thieving is degrading according to the character of the theft; begging is degrading but it is not as undignified as drunkenness. In all our vices we are aware of our degradation; but in drunkenness we lose our pride, our heads, and, above all, our natural dignity. We become so obviously and helplessly 'human', that we lose our glorious animal identity.

I sat down at the side of the bed, and bending over Suraj, whispered, 'I got drunk and lost fifty rupees, what am I to do about it?'

He smiled, but still he didn't open his eyes, and I kicked off my sandals and pulled off my shirt and lay down across the foot of the bed. He was still burning with fever, I could feel it radiating through the sheet.

We were silent for a long time, and I didn't know

if he was awake or asleep; so I pressed his foot and said, 'I'm sorry,' but he was asleep now, and did not hear me.

Moonlight.

Pipalnagar looks clean in the moonlight, and my thoughts are different from my daytime thoughts.

The streets are empty, and the moon probes the alleyways, and there is a silver dustbin, and even the slush and the puddles near the bus stop shimmer and glisten.

Kisses in the moonlight. Hungry kisses. The shudder of bodies clinging to each other on the moonswept floor.

A drunken quarrel in the street. Voices rise and fall. The night-watchman waits for the trouble to pass, and then patrols the street once more, banging the lathi on the pavement.

Kamla asleep. She sleeps like an angel. I go downstairs and walk in the moonlight. I meet Suraj coming home, his books under his arm; he has been studying late with Aziz, who has a junk shop near the station. Their exams are only a month off. I am confident that Suraj will be successful. I am only afraid that he will work himself to a standstill. With his weak chest and the uncertainty of his fits, he should not walk all day and read all night.

When I wake in the early hours of the morning and Kamla stirs beside me in the sleep (her hair so laden with perfume that my own sleep has been fitful and disturbed), Suraj is still squatting on the floor, reading by the light of the kerosene lamp.

And even when he has finished reading, he does not sleep, but asks me to walk with him before the sun rises. And, as women were not made to get up before the sun, we leave Kamla stretched out on the cot, relaxed and languid; small breasts and a boy's waist; her hair tumbling about the pillow; her mouth slightly apart, her lips still swollen and bruised with kisses.

I have been seeking through sex something beyond sex—a union with all mankind.

# The Sensualist

'One evening, I pushed open the door of an old house teetering over the riverbank, and looked into a narrow passage dimly lighted by a green paper lantern. From within came the sounds of flute and sitar. A curtain was drawn back and an old woman came towards me. She was a withered old crone who glanced at me with an enticing leer and led me to the top of a staircase where she took my money with a swooping, gull-like movement. She then led me into a small, dark room where I was able to make out a wide couch, raised just above the floor and decorated with a gay but tattered rug.

'"I will fetch Shankhini for you," she said. "You will be happy with her."

'My eyes gradually grew accustomed to the dim light, and I was able to see the girl who entered the room and closed and bolted the door behind her. She drew near with a composed and friendly manner, as if I was an old acquaintance. And in some ways I suppose I must have been, for to the prostitute, all men are one—unity in diversity!

Extract from *The Sensualist: A Cautionary Tale*

'Except for a diaphanous wrap of silk and a narrow girdle, the girl was completely naked. She wore white jasmine blossoms in her black hair. She looked little more than a child, although her hips were graceful and well-rounded.

'"Shall I dance?" she asked. "Tell me what you would like me to do."

'"Dance," I said. I had been unprepared for her youthfulness.

'And so she danced beneath the greenish moon of the paper lantern, and the only sound was the soft fall of her feet upon the mat. The heavy door shut out the music downstairs, the street cries, the hollow boom of the river. It was a dance without music, without sound, and I felt as though those small feet were dancing gently on my heart, on the very source of my life. When the dancing ceased, the girl smiled at me with an expression simultaneously wise, childlike, and passionate. Looking like a sleek green-gold cat in the light from the lantern, she subsided softly on the couch beside me. She had been trained in the art of making love. And yet beneath it all lay an undercurrent of innocence. I think this was because she suffered from no feelings of guilt. She had been brought up to please men as though this was her sole duty in life. She had not known and did not seek any other kind of existence.

'She did not let a moment pass in which she did not seem to be giving herself. Her aspect was continually changing. She did not surrender even one of her secrets without giving me an inkling that another still remained to be disclosed.

'"Do you find me beautiful?" she asked. It was her stock question. And I gave her the expected answer, "You are the most beautiful girl I have ever seen."

'She smiled at me with her large, childlike eyes. Then her head came between me and the lantern, and her face seemed to be framed in a halo of green light.

'"Forget everything," she said. "Here there is no time, neither night nor day."

'"Let me do something for you," I said, feeling suddenly generous towards this girl. "Let me give you something."

'"I take nothing," she answered. "It is for the old woman to take. You must only tell me that I am beautiful and that I have made you happy."

'"You are very beautiful. You make me very happy."

'"I have heard it a hundred times. But I still like to hear it." And then, drawing close to me and gazing into my eyes, she said, "You are very important to yourself, are you not?" She raised her hand to my brow, and tapping my temples with her painted fingers, said, "There is a cold fire there! It is stronger than all other flames, and seems brighter. It fights against the warmth of the heart, and will quench the fire of many hearts. So you must always move from one to another. What are you looking for? There is nothing to find. Forget everything. Love me, and forget!"

'Forget? Can the mind forget? It was written by a sage of old, "Remember past deeds, O my mind, remember!" But the injunction is unnecessary, because we are remembering all the time—even when we say we have forgotten. And can the memory of past deeds really shape the nature of future deeds? Man cannot help but live in conformity with his nature; his subconscious is more powerful than his conscious mind, and he cannot deny his body until he removes himself from the scene of all physical activity. It is useless to struggle against one's nature. Some believe that there is salvation in struggle—they are merely showing that they do not know what salvation is.

'At first I sought to assuage my restlessness by communing with nature. I searched for truth in the rippling of streams and the rustling of leaves; in the blue heavens or the wilderness of the jungle; in the behaviour of men, beasts and plants; in the superabundance of sunshine that pours down in India. But our bodies germinate as the resurrections of nature. Each bubbling spring, swelling fruit or bursting blossom, reminded me that I too was part of this burgeoning process, so that it was not long before the throb in my loins was as tenderly painful as the unfolding of a rosebud.

'I am not trying to give you the impression that those years of youthful dissipation were interspersed with a vague searching for my inner self. Once again, I have anticipated . . . The search, if you can call it that, came later. I am merely trying to tell you how I came to be here. This cave is the end of all searching, but before the search there was the indulgence, and the indulgence was a part of the process that brought me to this place.'

'And, meanwhile, I grew in Mulia's love.'

'She tended me as a gardener tends a favourite plant, giving it all the water and nourishment it needs. Special sweets were made for me. Ancient recipes were turned up, and sherbets of many hues and flavours were given to me morning, noon and night. I had given up asking what they contained. I left everything to Mulia. She tried each potion before passing it to me, to make sure that the brew was not too potent. I was convinced that one day I would find her lying dead on the floor, poisoned by one of her own concoctions.

'But I was not the sort of person who could give anything in return for love. As soon as I found someone growing tender towards me, I withdrew into myself, became remote and cold, so that the love that might have been mine was squandered in an empty void. I was determined to leave them with a feeling of insufficiency. Those who gave themselves to me suffered for it. I became cruel and callous towards them. Was it victory I wanted, or the chance to spurn victory? Samyukta was made to suffer in this way. But Mulia, twenty years older than me, was an exception. I seldom withheld my affections from her, I knew that she was wholly for me and with me. My wealth, strength, welfare and happiness were her sole concern. I was the ruling passion of her life and I knew that if I was taken from her, she would lose the impetus for living.

'Shankhini, the woman who lived by night, was in a different category altogether. All men had immersed themselves in her, and she could not be expected to love an individual man any more, than a man could be expected to love her. But what was the mysterious attraction that drew me back to her again and again? She had no hold over me. And the old crone who ran the house, certain that I was enamoured with the lithe and boyish figure of this unusual girl, put the price up at every visit. I did not care, I could afford it—or rather my father could afford it. It even gave me a sensuous thrill to hand over the money to the old woman. Not that the old woman excited me in any way; she would have found it hard to arouse a camel! But the business of handing over the money in exchange for an hour or two of personal possession, ownership, of the girl who lived always in green shadows, was a thrill in itself.

'But would I ever be able to arouse her to any degree of rapture? Although I restrained myself, and took the time and trouble to create in her some crisis of response, she seemed incapable of reaching a state of ecstasy and abandonment. There had been too many men, she told me. Coupling with them had become a mechanical process, and there was no intensity or pleasurable sensation in it. She went through the motions, expertly and in order to satisfy those who had paid for the pastime, but she could not be expected to enjoy the game herself.'

'So perhaps she was a challenge to me, and that was why I went to her. I wanted to elicit from her a genuine, not a trained response. I think she preferred me to most of her customers, many of whom were pot-bellied businessmen whose overburdened waistlines gave their manhood a shrivelled aspect. Obesity is not conducive to effective lovemaking.

'It may seem strange, but I liked to talk to Shankhini. In those days, there were few to whom I could talk freely. Mulia was illiterate, and her talk was confined to practical affairs, my needs and bodily functions. She had no other interest outside her small world of service. My mother was old-fashioned and superstitious and so we had very little to say to each other. I hardly ever saw my father. Fellow students at school and college considered me a snob, a wealthy aristocrat, a privileged member of a feudal society. They envied me, and were a little afraid of me too, because unlike others from affluent families, I made no attempt to ingratiate myself with them. Had I lavished money on a few young men, I would soon have had a following, but I had no need of sycophants. I could live with myself, and within myself, provided there were always these women to bear the burden of my ego.

'Samyukta was intelligent, but there was no real meeting of our minds—the relationship was purely sensual in nature. I gave her the satisfaction she needed after she had exhausted herself intellectually. She was studying medicine, and had to work very hard. Whenever she stopped working, she wanted to stop thinking. I could supply no intellectual need, nor was that what she wanted. But when I moved within her, she cried with ecstasy, she was convulsed with joy; but afterwards she had little or nothing to say. She turned over, lay flat on her belly, and slept.

'And so in the evenings, as the lights were lit in the bazaar, and pilgrims placed little leaf-boats filled with rose petals on the waters of the river, I made my way to the tall old house with the green paper lanterns, and asked for Shankhini.

'She was not always available in the evenings. So I took to visiting her in the afternoons, when other men were busy earning a living.

'The old woman told Shankhini I paid well, and so she went out of her way to make me comfortable, to please me, and to persuade me to come again. She did this as part of her duty; but it wasn't all commercial enterprise. As familiarity grew between us, we spent some time in talk. What did we have to say to each other? I don't remember much of it, but this strange girl had evolved a philosophy of her own to deal with the situation she found herself in. It was all a question of doing one's duty, she said. Death was a duty, just as much as life was just another way of dying.'

# Miss Bun and Others

*1 March 1975*

Beer in the sun. High in the spruce tree the barbet calls, heralding summer. A few puffy clouds drift lazily over the mountains. Is this the great escape?

I could sit here all day, soaking up beer and sunshine, but at *some* time during the day I must wipe the dust from my typewriter and produce something readable. There's only Rs 800 in the bank, book sales are falling off, and magazines are turning away from fiction.

Prem spoils me, gives me rice and kofta curry for lunch, which means that I sleep till four when Miss Bun arrives with patties and samosas.

Miss Bun is the baker's daughter.

Of course that's not her real name. Her real name is very long and beautiful, but I won't give it here for obvious reasons and also because her brother is big and ugly.

I am seeing Miss Bun after two months. She's been with relatives in Bareilly.

She sits at the foot of my bed, absolutely radiant. Her raven-black hair lies loose on her shoulders; her eyelashes have been trimmed and blackened; so have her eyes, with kajal. Her eyes, so large and innocent—and calculating!

There are pretty glass bangles on her wrists and she wears a pair of new slippers. Her kameez is new, too; green silk, with gold-embroidered sleeves.

'You must have a rich lover,' I remark, taking her hand and gently pulling her towards me. 'Who gave you all this finery?'

'You did. Don't you remember? Before I went away, you gave me a hundred rupees.'

'That was for the train and bus fares I thought.'

'Oh, my uncle paid the fares. So I bought myself these things. Are they nice?'

'Very pretty. And so are you. If you were ten years older, and I was ten years younger, we'd make a good pair. But, I'd have been broke long before this!'

She giggles and drops a paper bag full of samosas on the bedside table. I hate samosas and patties, but I keep ordering them because it gives Miss Bun a pretext for visiting me. It's all in the way of helping the bakery get by. When she goes, I give the lot to Bijju and Binya or whoever might be passing.

'You've been away a long time,' I complain.

'What if I'd got married while you were away?'

'Then you'd stop ordering samosas.'

'Or get them from that old man Bashir, who makes much better ones, and cheaper!'

She drops her head on my shoulder. Her hair is heavily scented with jasmine hair oil, and I nearly pass out. They should use it instead of anaesthesia.

'You smell very nice,' I lie. 'Do I get a kiss?'

She gives me a long kiss, as though to make up for her long absence. Her kisses always have a nice wholesome flavour, as you would expect from someone who lives in a bakery.

'That was an expensive kiss.'

'I want to buy some face cream.'

'You don't need face cream. Your complexion is perfect. It must be the good quality flour you use in the bakery.'

'I don't put flour on my face. Anyway, I want the cream for my elder sister. She has pockmarks.'

I surrender and give her two fives, quickly putting away my wallet.

'And when will you pay for the samosas?'

'Next week.'

'I'll bring you something nice next week,' she says, pausing in the doorway.

'Well, thanks, I was getting tired of samosas.' She was gone in a twinkling.

I'll say this for Miss Bun: she doesn't take the trouble to hide her intentions.

*4 March*

My policeman calls on me this morning. Ghanshyam, the constable attached to the Barlowganj outpost.

He is not very tall for a policeman, and he has a round, cheerful countenance, which is unusual in his profession. He looks smart in his uniform. Most constables prefer to hang around in their pyjamas most of the time.

Nothing alarming about Ghanshyam's visit. He comes to see me about once a week, and has been doing so ever since I spent a night in the police station last year.

It happened when I punched a Muzzaffarnagar businessman in the eye for bullying a rickshaw coolie. The fat slob very naturally lodged a complaint against me, and that same evening a sub-inspector called and asked me to accompany him to the thana. It was too late to arrange anything and in any case I had only been taken in for questioning, so I had to spend the night at the police post. The sub-inspector went home and left me in the charge of a constable. A wooden bench and a charpoy were the only items of furniture in my 'cell', if you could call it that. The charpoy was meant for the night-duty constable, but he very generously offered it to me.

'But where will you sleep?' I asked.

'Oh, I don't feel like sleeping. Usually, I go to the night show at the Picture Palace, but I suppose I'll have to stay here because of you.'

He looked rather sulky. Obviously, I'd ruined his plans for the night.

'You don't have to stay because of me,' I said. 'I won't tell the SHO. You go to the Picture Palace, I'll look after the thana.'

He brightened up considerably, but still looked a bit doubtful.

'You can trust me,' I said encouragingly. 'My grandfather was a private soldier who became a Buddhist.'

'Then I can trust you as far as your grandfather.' He was quite cheerful now, and sent for two cups of tea from the shop across the road. It came gratis, of course. A little later he left me, and I settled down on the cot and slept fitfully. The constable came back during the early hours and went to sleep on the bench. Next morning I was allowed to go home. The Muzzaffarnagar businessman had got into another fight and was lodged in the main thana. I did not hear about the matter again.

Ghanshyam, the constable, having struck up a friendship with me, was to visit me from time to time.

And here he is today, boots shining, teeth gleaming, cheeks almost glowing, far too charming a person to be a policeman.

'Hello, Ghanshyam bhai,' I welcome him. 'Sit down and have some tea.'

'No, I can't stop for long,' he says, but sits down beside me on the veranda steps. 'Can you do me a favour?'

'Sure. What is it?'

'I'm fed up with Barlowganj. I want to get a transfer.'

'And how can I help you? I don't know any netas or bigwigs.'

'No, but our SP will be here next week, and he can have me transferred. Will you speak to him?'

'But why should he listen to me?'

'Well, you see, he has a weakness . . .'

'We all have our weaknesses. Does your SP have a weakness similar to mine? Do we proceed to blackmail him?'

'Yes. You see, he writes poetry. And you are a kavi, a poet, aren't you?'

'At times,' I concede. 'And I have to admit it's a weakness, specially as no one cares to read my poetry.'

'No one reads the SP's poetry, either. Although we have to listen to it sometimes. When he has finished reading out one of his poems, we salute and say "Shabash!"'

'A captive audience. I wish I had one.'

Ignoring my sarcasm, Ghanshyam continues, 'The trouble is, he can't get anyone to publish his poems. This makes him bad-tempered and unsympathetic to applications for transfer. Can you help?'

'I am not a publisher. I can only salute like the rest of you.'

'But you know publishers, don't you? If you can get some of his poems published, he'd be very grateful. To you. To me. To both of us!'

'You really are an optimist.'

'Just one or two poems. You see, I've already told him about you. How you spent all night in the lock-up writing verses. He thinks you are a famous writer. He's depending on me now. If the poems get published, he will give me a transfer. I'm sick of Barlowganj!' He gives me a hug and pinches me on the cheek. Before he can go any further, I say, 'Well, I'll do my best.' I am thinking of a little magazine published in Bhopal where most of my rejects find a home. 'For your sake, I'll try. But first I must see the poems.'

'You shall even see the SP,' he promises. 'I'll bring him here next week. You can give him a cup of tea.'

He gets up, gives me a smart salute, and goes up the path with a spring in his step. The sort of man who knows how to get his transfers and promotions in a perfectly honest manner.


7 *March*

It gets warmer day by day.

This morning I decided to sunbathe—quite modestly, of course. Retaining my old khaki shorts but removing all other clothing, I stretched out on a mattress in the garden. Almost immediately, I was disturbed by the baker (Miss Bun's father for a change), who presented me with two loaves of bread and half a dozen chocolate pastries, ordered the previous day. Then Prem's small son, Raki, turned up, demanding a pastry, and I gave him two. He insisted on joining me on the mattress, where he proceeded to drop crumbs in my hair and on my chest. '*Good* morning, Mr Bond!' came the dulcet tones of Mrs Biggs, leaning over the gate. Forgetting that she was short-sighted, I jumped to my feet, and at the same time my shorts slipped down over my knees. As I grabbed for them, Mrs Biggs's effusiveness reached greater heights. 'Why, what a lovely *agapanthus* you've got!' she exclaimed, referring no doubt to the solitary lily in the garden. I must confess I blushed. Then, recovering myself, I returned her greeting, remarking on the freshness of the morning.

Mrs Biggs, at eighty, is a little deaf as well, and replied, 'I'm very well, thank you, Mr Bond. Is that a child you're carrying?'

'Yes, Prem's small son.'

'Prem is your son? I didn't know you had a family.'

At this point Raki decided to pluck the

spectacles off Mrs Biggs's nose, and after I had recovered them for her, she beat a hasty retreat.

Later, the Rev. Mr Biggs comes over to borrow a book. 'Just light reading,' he says. 'I can't concentrate for long periods.'

He has become extremely absent-minded and forgetful; one of the drawbacks of living to an advanced age. During a funeral last year, at which he took the funeral service, he read out the service for Burial at Sea. It was raining heavily at the time, and no one seemed to notice.

Now he borrows two of my Ross Macdonalds—the same two he read last month. I refrain from pointing this out. If he has forgotten the books already, it won't matter if he reads them again.

Having spent the better part of his seventy-odd years in India, the Rev. Biggs has a lot of stories to tell, his favourite being the one about the crocodile he shot in Orissa when he was a young man. He'd pitched his tent on the banks of a river and had gone to sleep on a camp cot. During the night, he felt his cot moving, and before he could gather his wits, the cot had moved swiftly through the opening of the tent and was rapidly making its way down to the river. Mr Biggs leapt for dry land while the cot, firmly wedged on the back of the crocodile, disappeared into the darkness.

Crocodiles, it seems, often bury themselves in the mud when they go to sleep, and Mr Biggs had pitched his tent and made his bed on top of a sleeping crocodile. Waking in the night, it had made for the nearest water.

Mr Biggs shot it the following morning—or so he would have us believe—the crocodile having reappeared on the river bank with the cot still attached to its back.

Now, having told me this story for the umpteenth time, Biggs says he really must be going, and, returning to the bookshelf, extracts Gibbons' *Decline and Fall of the Roman Empire*, having forgotten the Ross Macdonalds on a side table.

'I must do some serious reading,' he says. 'These modern novels are so violent.'

'Lots of violence in *Decline and Fall*,' I remark.

'Ah, but it's history, isn't it? Well, I must go now, Mr Macdonald. Mustn't waste your time.'

As he steps outside, he collides with Miss Bun, who drops samosas all over the veranda steps.

'Oh, dear, I'm so sorry,' he apologizes, and

starts picking up the samosas, despite my attempts to prevent him from doing so. He then takes the paper bag from Miss Bun and replaces the samosas.

'And who is this little girl?' he said benignly, patting Miss Bun on the head. 'One of your nieces?'

'That's right, sir. My favourite niece.'

'Well, I must not keep you. Service as usual, on Sunday.' 'Right, Mr Biggs.'

I have never been to a local church service, but why disillusion Rev. Biggs? I shall defend everyone's right to go to a place of worship provided they allow me the freedom to stay away.

Miss Bun is staring after Rev. Biggs as he crosses the road. Her mouth is slightly agape. 'What's the matter?' I ask.

'He's taken all the samosas!'

When I kiss Miss Bun, she bites my lip and draws blood.

'What was that for?' I complain.

'Just to make you angry.'

'But I don't like getting angry.'

'That's why.'

I get angry just to please her, and we take a tumble on the carpet.

*19 March*

Vinod, now selling newspapers, arrives as I am pouring myself a beer under the cherry tree. It's a warm day and I can see he is thirsty.

'Can I have a drink of water?' he asks.

'Would you like some beer?'

'Yes, *sir*!'

As I have an extra bottle, I pour him a glass and he squats on the grass near the old wall and brings me up to date on the local gossip. There are about fifty papers in his shoulder-bag, yet to be delivered.

'You may feel drowsy after some time,' I warn. 'Don't leave your papers in the wrong houses.'

'Nothing to worry about,' he says, emptying the glass and gazing fondly at the bottle sparkling in the spring sunshine.

'Have some more,' I tell him, and go indoors to see what Prem is making for lunch. (Stuffed gourds, fried brinjal slices, pillau rice. Prem was in a good mood, preparing my favourite dishes. Had I upset him, he would have given me string beans.) Returning to the garden, I find Vinod well into his second glass of beer. Half of Barlowganj and all of Jharipani (the next village), are snarling and cursing, waiting for their newspapers.

'Your customers must be getting impatient,' I remark. 'Surely they want to know the result of the cricket test.'

'Oh, they heard it on the radio. This is the morning edition. I can deliver it in the evening.'

I go indoors and have my lunch with little Raki, and ask Prem to give Vinod something to eat. When I come outside again, he is stretched out under the cherry tree, burping contentedly.

'Thank you for the lunch,' he says, and closes his eyes and goes to sleep.

He's gone by the evening but his bag of papers is resting against my front door.

'He's left his papers behind,' I remark to Prem.

'Oh, he'll deliver them tomorrow, along with tomorrow's paper. He'll say the mail-bus was late, due to a landslide.'

In the evening I walk through the old bazaar and linger in front of a Tibetan shop, gazing at the brassware, coloured stones, amulets, masks. I am about to pass on, when I catch a glimpse of the girl who looks after the shop. Two soft brown eyes in a round jade-smooth face. A hesitant smile.

I step inside. I have never cared much for

Tibetan handicrafts, but beautiful jade eyes are different.

*31 March*

Miss Bun hasn't been for several days. This morning I find her washing clothes at the public tap. She gives me a quick smile as I pass.

'It's nice to see you hard at work,' I remark.

She looks quickly to the left and the right, then says, 'It's punishment, because I bought new bangles with the money you gave me.'

I hurry on down the road.

During the afternoon siesta I am roused by someone knocking on the door. A slim boy, with thick hair and bushy eyebrows, is standing there. I don't know him, but his eyes remind me of someone.

He tells me he is Miss Bun's older brother. At a guess, he would be only a year or two older than her.

'Come in,' I say. It's best to be friendly! What could he possibly want?

He produces a bag of samosas and puts them down on my bedside table.

'My sister cannot come this week. I will bring you samosas instead. Is that all right?'

'Oh, sure. Sit down, sit down. So you're Master Bun. It's nice to know you.'

He sits down on the edge of the bed and studies the picture on the wall—a print of Kurosawa's *Wave*.

'Shall I pay you now for the samosas?' I ask.

'No, no, whenever you like.'

'And do you go to school or college?'

'No, I help my father in the bakery. Are you ill, sir?'

'No. What makes you think so?'

'Because you were lying down.'

'Well, I like lying down. It's better than standing up. And I do get a headache if I read or write for too long.'

He offers to give me a head massage, and I submit to his ministrations for about five minutes. The headache is now much worse, but I pay for both the massage and samosas and tell him he can come again—preferably next year.

My next visitor is Constable Ghanshyam Singh, who tells me that the SP has extracted confessions from a couple of thieves simply by making them stand for hours and listen to him reciting his poetry. I know our police have a reputation for torturing suspects, but I think this is carrying things a bit too far.

'And what about your transfer?' I ask.

'As soon as those poems are published in the *Weekly*.'

'I'll do my best,' I promise.

They appeared in the Bhopal *Weekly*.

And a year later, when I was editing *Imprint*, I was able to publish one of the SP's poems. He has always maintained that if I'd published more of them, the magazine would never have folded.

A note on Miss Bun:

> *Little Miss Bun is fond of bed,*
> *But she keeps a cash box in her head.*

*8 April*

Rev. Biggs at the door, book in hand.

'I won't take up your time, Mr Bond. But I thought it was time I returned your butterfly book.'

'My butterfly book?'

'Yes, thank you very much. I enjoyed it a great deal.'

Mr Biggs hands me the book on butterflies, a handsomely illustrated volume. It isn't my book, but if Mr Biggs insists on giving me someone else's book, who am I to quibble? He'd never find the right owner, anyway.

'By the way, have you seen Mrs Biggs?' he asks.

'No, not this morning, sir.'

'She went off without telling me. She's always doing things like that. Very irritating.'

After he has gone, I glance at the flyleaf of the book. The nameplate says W. Biggs. So it's one of his own . . .

A little later Mrs Biggs comes by.

'Have you seen Will?' she asks.

'He was here about fifteen minutes ago. He was looking for you.'

'Oh, he knew I'd gone to the garden shed. How tiresome! I suppose he's wandered off somewhere.'

'Never mind, Mrs Biggs, he'll make his way home when he gets hungry. A good lunch will always bring a wanderer home. By the way, I've got his book on butterflies. Perhaps you'd return it to him for me? And he shouldn't lend it to just anyone, you know. It's a valuable book, you don't want to lose it.'

'I'm sure it was quite safe with you, Mr Bond.'

Books always are, of course. On principle, I

never steal another man's books. I might take his geraniums or his old school tie, but I wouldn't deprive him of his books. Or the song or melody or dream he lives by.

And later, in the evening, I wrote a little lullaby for Raki.


*16 April*

Visited the Tibetan shop and bought a small brass vase encrusted with pretty stones.

I'd no intention of buying anything, but the girl smiled at me as I passed, and then I just had to go in; and once in, I couldn't just stand there, a fatuous grin on my face.

I had to buy something. And a vase is always a good thing to buy. If you don't like it, you can give it away.

If she smiles at me every time I pass, I shall probably build up a collection of vases.

She isn't a girl, really; she's probably about thirty. I suppose she has a husband who smuggles Chinese goods in from Nepal, while her children—'charity cases'—go to one of the posh public schools; but she's fresh and pretty, and then, of course, I don't have many young women smiling at me these days. I shall be forty-three next month.

*17 April*

Miss Bun still smiles at me, even though I frown at her when we pass.

This afternoon she brought me samosas and a rose.

'Where's your brother?' I asked gruffly. 'He has more to talk about.'

'He's busy in the bakery. See, I've brought you a rose.'

'How much did it cost?'

'Don't be silly. It's a present.'

'Thanks. I didn't know you grew roses.'

'I don't. It's from the school garden.'

'Well, thank you anyway. You actually stole something on my behalf!'

'Where shall I put it?'

I found my new vase, filled it with fresh water, placed the rose in it, and set it down on my dressing table.

'It leaks,' remarked Miss Bun.

'My vase?' I was incredulous.

'See, the water's spreading all over your nice table.'

She was right, of course. Water from the bottom of the vase was running across the varnished wood of great-grandmother's old rosewood dressing table. The stain, I felt sure, would be permanent.

'But it's a new vase!' I protested.

'Someone must have cheated you. Why did you buy it without looking properly?'

'Well, you see, I didn't buy it actually. Someone gave it to me as a present.'

I fumed inwardly, vowing never again to visit the brassware shop. Never trust a smiling woman! I prefer Miss Bun's scowl.

'Do you want the vase?' she asked.

'No. Take it away.'

She placed the rose on my pillow, threw the water out of the window, and dropped the vase into her cloth shopping-bag.

'What will you do with it?' I asked.

'I'll seal the leak with flour,' she said.

*21 April*

A clear fresh morning after a week of intermittent rain. And what a morning for birds! Three doves acourting, a cuckoo calling, a bunch of mynas squabbling, and a pair of king-crows doing

Swedish exercises.

I find myself doing exercises of an original nature, devised by Master Bun; these consist of various contortions of the limbs which, he says, are good for my sex drive.

'But I don't want a sex drive,' I tell him. 'I want something that will take my mind *off* sex.'

So he gives me another set of exercises, which consist mostly of deep breathing.

'Try holding your breath for five minutes,' he suggests.

'I know of someone who committed suicide by doing just that.'

'Then hold it for two minutes.'

I take a deep breath and last only a minute.

'No good,' he says. 'You have to relax more.'

'Well, I am tired of trying to relax. It doesn't work this way. What I need is a good meal.'

And Prem obliges by serving up my favourite kofta curry and rice. Satiated, I have no problem in relaxing for the rest of the afternoon.

*28 April*

Master Bun wears a troubled expression.

'It's about my sister,' he says.

'What about her?' I ask, fearing the worst.

'She has run away.'

'That's bad. On her own?'

'No . . . With a professor.'

'That should be all right. Professors are usually respectable people. Maths or English?'

'I don't know. He has a wife and children.'

'Then obviously he hasn't taken them along.'

'He has taken her to Roorkee. My sister is an innocent girl.'

'Well, there is a certain innocence about her,' I say, recalling Nabokov's *Lolita*. 'Maybe the professor wants to adopt her.'

'But she's a virgin.'

'Then she must be rescued! Why are you here, talking to me about it, when you should be rushing down to Roorkee?'

'That's why I've come. Can you lend me the bus fare?'

'Better still, I'll come with you. We must rescue the professor—sorry, I mean your sister!'

*1 May*

*To Roorkee, to Roorkee, to find a sweet girl,*
*Home again, home again, oh what a whirl!*

We did everything except find Miss Bun. Our first evening in Roorkee we roamed the bazaar and the canal banks; the second day we did the rounds of the University, the regimental barracks, and the headquarters of the Boys' Brigade. We made inquiries from all the bakers in Roorkee (many of them known to Master Bun), but none of them had seen his sister. On the college campus, we asked for the professor, but no one had heard of him either.

Finally, we bought platform tickets and sat down on a bench at the end of the railway platform and watched the arrivals and departures of trains, and the people who got on and off. We saw no one who looked in the least like Miss Bun. Master Bun bought an astrological guide from the station bookstall, and studied his sister's horoscope to see if that might help, but it didn't. At the same bookstall, hidden under a pile of pirated Harold Robbins novels, I found a book of mine that had been published ten years earlier. No one had bought it in all that time. I replaced it at the top of the pile. Never lose hope!

On the third day we returned to Barlowganj and found Miss Bun at home.

She had gone no further than Dehra's Paltan

Bazaar, it seemed, and had ditched the professor there, having first made him buy her three dress pieces, two pairs of sandals, a sandalwood hair brush, a bottle of scent, and a satchel for her schoolbooks.

## 5 May

And now it's Mr Biggs's turn to disappear.

'Have you seen our Will?' asks Mrs Biggs at my gate.

'Not this morning, Mrs Biggs.'

'I can't find him anywhere. At breakfast he said he was going out for a walk, but nobody knows where he went, and he isn't in the school compound, I've just inquired. He's been gone over three hours!'

'Don't worry, Mrs Biggs. He'll turn up. Someone on the hillside must have asked him in for a cup of tea, and he's sitting there talking about the crocodile he shot in Orissa.'

But at lunchtime Mr Biggs hadn't returned; and that was alarming, because Mr Biggs had never been known to miss his favourite egg curry and pillau rice.

We organized a search. Prem and I walked the length of the Barlowganj bazaar, and even lodged an unofficial report with Constable Ghanshyam. No one had seen him in the bazaar. Several members of the school staff combed the hillside without picking up the scent.

Mid-afternoon, while giving my negative report to Mrs Biggs, I heard a loud thumping coming from the direction of her storeroom.

'What's all that noise downstairs?' I asked.

'Probably rats. I don't hear anything.'

I ran downstairs and opened the storeroom door, there was Mr Biggs looking very dusty and very disgruntled; he wanted to know why the devil (the first time he'd taken the devil's name in vain), Mrs Biggs had shut him up for hours. He'd gone into the storeroom in search of an old walking stick, and Mrs Biggs, seeing the door open, had promptly bolted it, failing to hear her husband's cries for immediate release. But for Mr Bond's presence of mind, he averred, he might have been discovered years later, a mere skeleton!

The cook was still out hunting for him, so Mr Biggs had his egg curry cold. Still in a foul mood, he sat down and wrote a letter to his sister in Turnbridge Wells, asking her to send a hearing aid for Mrs Biggs.

Constable Ghanshyam turned up in the evening, to inform me that Mr Biggs had last been seen at Rajpur, in the foothills, in the company of several gypsies!

'Never mind,' I said. 'These old men get that way. One last fling, one last romantic escapade, one last tilt at the windmill. If you have a dream, Ghanshyam, don't let them take it away from you.'

He looked puzzled, but went on to tell me that he was being transferred to Bareilly jail, where they keep those who have been found guilty but of unsound mind. It's a reward, no doubt, for his services in getting the SP's poems published.

These journal entries date back some twenty years. What happened to Miss Bun? Well, she finally opened a beauty parlour in New Delhi, but I still can't tell you where it is, or give you her name.

Two or three years later, Mrs Biggs was laid to rest near her old friends in the Mussoorie cemetery. Rev. Biggs was flown home to Turnbridge Wells; his sister gave him a solid tombstone, so that he wasn't tempted to get up and wander off somewhere, in search of crocodiles.

A lot can happen in twenty years, and,

unfortunately, not all of it gets recorded. Little Raki is today a married man!

# HH

*2nd June*

Drinks in the evening with HH and Bill. Dear HH ('Her Highness' of yore) is great fun over a few drinks, specially when she gets going on all the disasters that have overtaken her friends and acquaintances: P was knocked down by a truck; Y was sucked into the fuselage of an aeroplane; T has succumbed to an overdose of drugs and alcohol . . . She gives an excellent description of old S, a retired mountaineer, suffering from Alzheimer's and searching for Annapurna base camp on the Delhi Ridge. All with great sympathy and yet a certain relish. Anyone who is someone in Delhi now goes to a psychiatrist, she tells me, including one of her golfing friends, Mrs B, who is convinced that in her former life she was a golf ball.

As far as I can recall, Delhi did not have a single psychiatrist thirty years ago. No one was rich enough to afford such a luxury. Or perhaps no one was nutty enough. Now there are hundreds of psychiatrists, and thousands of affluent patients

---

Extract from *Leaves from a Journal*

who imagine they were once Mughal emperors, famous courtesans, Ming vases, or golf balls.

## 25th June

Visited HH and got news of fresh disasters:

1. Large number of tourists down with food poisoning after dining at a new hotel.

2. Abnormal nephew talks to the wall and flaps his arms like a bird. (I feel like doing this myself, sometimes.)

3. Young Prem lala, who fell off a roof and damaged his spine and skull, may never recover. (Six months later: I'm glad to be able to say that he did.)

I had gone over looking for something to cheer me up, but even Bill looked gloomy and his purple socks failed to stimulate.

## 21st July

Jolly evening at HH's in spite of the news that her grand-nephew was in a mental hospital, her business partner (in Bombay) was dying from lymph cancer, and almost every acquaintance was either expiring or in a bad way financially

She is, of course, immune to all the disasters that

surround her. Is fond of me but would never give me any money because she says I would squander it. And, of course, she's right—I would!

Ganesh did her a service, so she has promised him a new car. That is, if Nandu (of the Savoy) pays half.

### 6th September

Three days of incessant rain. A powdery film of mildew covers the frayed old carpet in the Savoy Bar; it is now as green as the billiard table. A fusty, musty odour pervades the airless room. Ganesh and I do our best to imbue it with some life. There have been no visitors for days, unless you count the little shrew that meanders between the chairs and tables. People say the shrew (chhuchhunder) is lucky, or rather, brings luck. Maybe I'll take it home one of these days. Nandu says to leave it—his need is greater than mine.

To relieve the tedium, we visit HH who has already informed me (on the phone) that she is severely depressed by Princess Diana's funeral which she has been following on TV. We find her cheerful enough, and she enlarges on her favourite theme of violent death, giving us tales of murder, suicide and misadventure in various princely families she has known. Poisonings were popular, followed by 'hunting' accidents.

Today, violent crime has shifted to political, business and entertainment circles. And poisonings and accidental deaths are passé. You simply contact a gang of hired killers (or kidnappers) who do the job for you. Rates are negotiable. And, of course, you might end up as one of their victims one day.

We shall miss HH when she leaves next week.

Speaking of an old flame, she remarks, 'It was Y—who taught me to drink.'

'And you were a quick learner,' adds Bill.

For which remark he will have to hide in the shrubbery for a day.


*15th September*
Glorious hot sunshine greets us this morning, and I resolve to do nothing but bask in it.

Twelve noon: Resolve has been undertaken.

One p.m.: Clouds move in.

Thought HH had gone, but received a merry call from her to say goodbye once again and to continue, 'Let me tell you about the latest tragedies that have taken place.'

First, Bill's mother had died, as well as one of his aunts, but as they were both over ninety, Bill wasn't too upset.

Second, her caretaker's TB treatment in Delhi had cost over ten thousand rupees and he still had the disease!

In spite of the recent horrendous train accident, HH is travelling by train to Delhi. Look forward to seeing her next year.

# The Old Lama

I meet him on the road every morning, on my walk up to the Landour post office. He's a lean, old man in a long maroon robe, a Tibetan monk of uncertain age. I'm told he's about eighty-five. But age is really immaterial in the mountains. Some grow old at their mother's breasts, and there are others who do not age at all.

If you are like this old lama, you go on forever. For he is a walking man, and there is no way you can stop him from walking.

The lama in Rudyard Kipling's *Kim*, rejuvenated by the mountain air, strode along with 'steady, driving strokes', leaving his disciple far behind. My lama, older and feebler than Kim's, walks very slowly, with the aid of an old walnut walking stick. The ferrule keeps coming off the end of the stick, but he puts it back with coal tar, left behind by the road repairers.

He plods and shuffles along. In fact, he's very like the tortoise in the story of the hare and the tortoise. I see him walking past my window, and five minutes later when I start out on the same road, I feel sure of overtaking him halfway up the hill. But invariably I find him standing near the post office when I get there.

He smiles when he sees me. We are always smiling at each other. His English is limited, and I speak absolutely no Tibetan. He knows a few words of Hindi, enough to make his needs known, but that's about all. He is quite happy to converse silently with all the creatures and people who take notice of him on the road.

It's the same walk he takes every morning. At 9 o'clock, if I look out of my window, I can see a line of Tibetan prayer flags fluttering over an old building in the cantonment. He emerges from beneath the flags and starts up the steep road. Ten minutes later, he is below my window, and sometimes he stops to sit and rest on my steps, or on a parapet farther along the road. Sooner or later, coming or going, I shall pass him on the road or up near the post office. His eyes will twinkle behind thick-lensed glasses, and he will raise his walking stick slightly in salutation. If I say something to him, he just smiles and nods vigorously in agreement.

An agreeable man.

He was one of those who came to India in 1959, fleeing the Chinese occupation of Tibet. The Dalai

Lama found sanctuary in India, and lived here in Mussoorie for a couple of years; many of his followers settled here. A new generation of Tibetans has grown up in the hill station, and those under thirty years have never seen their homeland.

But for almost all of them, and there are several thousand in this district alone, Tibet is their country, their real home, and they are quick to express their determination to go back when their land is free again.

Even a twenty-year-old girl like Tseten, who has grown up knowing English and Hindi, speaks of the day when she will return to Tibet with her parents. She has given me a painting of Milarepa, the Buddhist monk-philosopher, meditating beneath a fruit-laden peace tree, the eternal snows in the background. This is, perhaps, her vision of the Tibet which she would like to see, some day. Meanwhile, she works as a typist in the office of the Tibetan Homes Foundation.

My old lama will, I am sure, be among the first to return, even if he has to walk all the way over the mountain passes. Maybe that's why he plods up and around this hill every day. He is practising for the long walk back to Tibet.

Here he is again, pausing at the foot of my steps. It's a cool, breezy morning, and he does not feel the need to sit down. '*Tashi-tilay*! Good day!' I greet him, in the only Tibetan I know.

'*Tashi-tilay*!' he responds, beaming with delight.

'Will you go back to Tibet one day?' I ask him for the first time.

In spite of his limited Hindi, he understands me immediately, and nods vigorously.

'Soon, soon!' he exclaims, and raises his walking stick to emphasize his words.

Yes, if the Tibetans are able to return to their country, he will be among the first to go back. His heart is still on that high plateau. And like the tortoise, he'll be there waiting for the young hares to catch up with him.

If he goes, I shall certainly miss him on my walks.

# Sitaram

Someone was getting married, and the wedding band, brought up on military marches, unwittingly broke into the *Funeral March*. And they played loud enough to wake the dead.

After a medley of Souza marches, they switched to Hindi film tunes, and Sitaram came in, flung his arms around, and shattered my eardrums with Talat Mehmood's latest love ballad. I responded with the *Volga Boatmen* in my best Nelson Eddy manner, and my landlady came running out of her shop downstairs, wanting to know if the washerman had strangled his wife or vice versa.

Anyway, it was to be a week of celebrations . . .

When I opened my eyes next day, it was to find a bright red geranium staring me in the face, accompanied by the aromatic odour of a crushed geranium leaf. Sitaram was thrusting a potted geranium at me and wishing me a happy birthday. I brushed a caterpillar from my pillow and sat up. Wordsworthian though I was in principle, I wasn't prepared for nature red in tooth and claw.

Extract from *A Handful of Nuts*

I picked up the caterpillar on its leaf and dropped it outside.

'Come back when you're a butterfly,' I said.

Sitaram had taken his morning bath and looked very fresh and spry. Unfortunately, he had doused his head with some jasmine-scented hair oil, and the room was reeking of it. Already a bee was buzzing around him.

'Thank you for the present,' I said. 'I've always wanted a geranium.'

'I wanted to bring a rose bush but the pot was too heavy.'

'Never mind. Geraniums do better on verandas.'

I placed the pot in a sunny corner of the small balcony, and it certainly did something for the place. There's nothing like a red geranium for bringing a balcony to life.

While we were about to plan the day's festivities, a stranger walked through my open door (one day, I'd have to shut it), and declared himself the inventor of a new flush-toilet which, he said, would revolutionize the sanitary habits of the town. We were still living in the thunderbox era, and only the very rich could afford Western-style lavatories. My visitor showed me diagrams of a seat which, he said, combined the best of East and West. You could squat on it, Indian-style, without putting too much strain on your abdominal muscles, and if you used water to wash your bottom, there was a little sprinkler attached which, correctly aimed, would do that job for you. It was comfortable, efficient, safe. Your effluent would be stored in a little tank, which could be detached when full, and emptied—where? He hadn't got around to that problem as yet, but he assured me that his invention had a great future.

'But why are you telling me all this?' I asked, 'I can't afford a fancy toilet seat.'

'No, no, I don't expect you to buy one.'

'You mean I should demonstrate?'

'Not at all. But you are a writer, I hear. I want a name for my new toilet seat. Can you help?'

'Why not call it the Sit-Safe?' I suggested.

'The Sit-Safe! How wonderful. Young Mr Bond, let me show my gratitude with a small present.' And he thrust a ten-rupee note into my hand and left the room before I could protest. 'It's definitely my birthday,' I said. 'Complete strangers walk in and give me money.'

'We can see three films with that,' said Sitaram.

'Or buy three bottles of beer,' I said.

But there were no more windfalls that morning, and I had to go to the old Allahabad Bank—where my grandmother had kept her savings until they had dwindled away—and withdraw one hundred rupees.

'Can you tell me my balance?' I asked Mr Jain, the elderly clerk who remembered my maternal grandmother.

'Two hundred and fifty rupees,' he said with a smile. 'Try to save something!'

I emerged into the hot sunshine and stood on the steps of the Bank, where I had stood as a small boy some fifteen years back, waiting for Granny to finish her work—I think she had been the only one in the family to put some money by for a rainy day—but these had been rainy days for her son and daughters and various fickle relatives who were always battening off her. Her own needs were few. She lived in one room of her house, leaving the rest of it for the family to use. When she died, the house was sold so that her children could once more go their impecunious ways.

I had no relatives to support, but here was William Matheson waiting for me under the old peepul tree. His hands were shaking.

'What's wrong?' I asked.

'Haven't had a cigarette for a week. Come on, buy me a packet of Charminar.'

Sitaram went out and bought samosas and jalebis and little cakes with icing made from solidified ghee. I fetched a few bottles of beer, some orangeades and lemonades and a syrupy cold drink called Vimto which was all the rage then. My landlady, hearing that I was throwing a party, sent me pakoras made with green chillies.

The party, when it happened, was something of an anticlimax.

Jai Shankar turned up promptly and ate all the jalebis. William arrived with Suresh Mathur, finished the beer, and demanded more.

Nobody paid much attention to Sitaram, he seemed so much at home. Caste didn't count for much in a fairly modern town, as Dehra was in those days. In any case, from the way Sitaram was strutting around, acting as though he owned the place, it was generally presumed that he was the landlady's son. He brought up a second relay of the lady's pakoras, hotter than the first lot, and they arrived just as the Maharani and Indu appeared in the doorway.

'Happy birthday, dear boy,' boomed the Maharani and seized the largest chilli pakora. Indu appeared behind her and gave me a box wrapped in gold and silver cellophane. I put it on my desk and hoped it contained chocolates, not studs and a tiepin.

The chilli pakoras did not take long to violate the Maharani's taste buds.

'Water, water!' she cried, and seeing the bathroom door open, made a dash for the tap.

Alas, the bathroom was the least attractive aspect of my flat. It had yet to be equipped with anything resembling the newly-invented Sit-Safe. But the lid of the thunderbox was fortunately down, as this particular safe hadn't been emptied for a couple of days. It was crowned by a rusty old tin mug. On the wall hung a towel that had seen better days. The remnants of a cake of Lifebuoy soap stood near a cracked washbasin. A lonely cockroach gave the Maharani a welcoming genuflection.

Taking all this in at a glance, she backed out, holding her hand to her mouth.

'Try a Vimto,' said William, holding out a bottle

gone warm and sticky.

'A glass of beer?' asked Jai Shankar.

The Maharani grabbed a glass of beer and swallowed it in one long gulp. She came up gasping, gave me a reproachful look—as though the chilli pakora had been intended for her—and said, 'Must go now. Just stopped by to greet you. Thank you very much—you must come to Indu's birthday party. *Next* year.'

Next year seemed a long way off.

'Thank you for the present,' I said.

And then they were gone, and I was left to entertain my cronies.

Suresh Mathur was demanding something stronger than beer, and as I felt that way myself, we trooped off to the Royal Cafe; all of us, except Sitaram, who had better things to do.

After two rounds of drinks, I'd gone through what remained of my money. And so I left William and Suresh to cadge drinks off one of the latter's clients, while I bid Jai Shankar goodbye on the edge of the parade ground. As it was still light, I did not have to see him home.

Some workmen were out on the parade ground, digging holes for tent pegs.

Two children were discussing the coming attraction.

'The circus is coming!'

'Is it big?'

'It's the biggest! Tigers, elephants, horses, chimpanzees! Tight-rope walkers, acrobats, strong men . . .'

'Is there a clown?'

'There has to be a clown. How can you have a circus without a clown?'

I hurried home to tell Sitaram about the circus. It would make a change from the cinema. The room had been tidied up, and the Maharani's present stood on my desk, still in its wrapper.

'Let's see what's inside,' I said, tearing open the packet.

It was a small box of nuts—almonds, pistachios, cashewnuts, along with a few dried figs.

'Just a handful of nuts,' said Sitaram, sampling a fig and screwing up his face.

I tried an almond, found it bitter and spat it out.

'Must have saved them from her wedding day,' said Sitaram.

'Appropriate in a way,' I said. 'Nuts for a bunch of nuts.'